THE CHILDREN

The Children's Machine

•••

RETHINKING SCHOOL IN THE AGE OF THE COMPUTER

•••

Seymour Papert

BasicBooks
A Division of HarperCollinsPublishers

Designed by Ellen Levine

Library of Congress Cataloging-in-Publication Data
Papert, Seymour.
     The children's machine: rethinking school in the age of the computer/Seymour Papert.
        p.   cm.
     Includes bibliographical references (p.) and index.
     ISBN 0–465–01830–0 (cloth)
     ISBN 0–465–01063–6 (paper)
     1. Computer assisted instruction. 2. Education—Data processing.
I. Title.
LB1028.5.P325   1992
371.3'34—dc20   91–59012
                                                                          CIP

98 97 96 95   RRD(H) 10 9 8 7 6 5

Contents

• , • •

Preface

● ● ●

IT is often said that we are entering the information age. This coming period could equally be called the age of learning: The sheer quantity of learning taking place in the world is already many times greater than in the past.

Not very long ago, and in many parts of the world even today, young people would learn skills they could use in their work throughout life. Today, in industrial countries, most people are doing jobs that did not exist when they were born. The most important skill determining a person's life pattern has already become the ability to learn new skills, to take in new concepts, to assess new situations, to deal with the unexpected. This will be increasingly true in the future: The competitive ability is the ability to learn.

What is true for individuals is even more true for nations. The competitive strength of a nation in the modern world is directly proportional to its learning capacity; that is, a combination of the learning capacities of the individuals and the institutions of the society.

Individual and institutional learning capacities do not always go together. For example, conditions in the Soviet Union bred a generation of individuals with a high degree of adaptability necessary for survival under the arbitrary oppression of the Communist regime. On the other hand, the breakdown of the institutions of the Soviet Union revealed an extraordinary degree of bureaucratic inflexibility. The institutions of the society were unable to "learn" to adapt to changing conditions; they were unable even to take account of the fact that a crisis was mounting until it had already reached fatal proportions.

Japan is the striking example in the contemporary world of a nation that has built success on the learning ability of the society—the capacity and willingness of its institutions and individuals to learn. Americans often complain that Japan has taken advantage of technical discoveries made in the United States. The complaint expresses my point perfectly, though in a sense opposite to the intentions of the complainers, who have failed to learn that the essence of the Japanese success is exactly the ability responsible for America's past successes—the willingness to learn. The complainers would do well to relearn from the Japanese the skill of learning, at which America was once the world's champion.

The rate of change in the workplace is not the only factor giving increased importance to the ability to learn. The global scale of the consequences of human actions makes it ever more urgent for us to understand what we are doing. The destruction of the upper atmosphere, the AIDS crisis, the population explosion, the social breakdown in American cities and Russian villages, the plight of the African continent, and all the other issues that make daily headlines are more than desperately urgent problems. They are examples of much worse to come if human beings cannot bring themselves, on a hitherto unprecedented scale, to learn new ways of thinking.

The optimistic note of this book comes from recognizing the potential synergy of two trends in the world. One of these trends is technological. The same technological revolution that has been responsible for the acute need for better learning also offers the means to take effective action. Information technologies, from television to computers and all their combinations, open unprecedented opportunities for action in improving the quality of the learning environment, by which I mean the whole set of conditions that contribute to shaping learning in work, in school, and in play.

The other trend is epistemological, a revolution in thinking about knowledge. The central thesis of this book is that the powerful contribution of the new technologies in the enhancement of learning is the creation of personal media capable of supporting a wide range of intellectual styles. Women and members of minority cultures have been most articulate in protesting the imposition of a single, uniform way of learning. Most have scarcely begun to use the new media to express and develop their particular voices. But it is children who have most visibly demonstrated the energizing effect of media that match their intellectual preferences. They have the most to gain and they have the most to give.

Across the world children have entered a passionate and enduring love affair with the computer. What they do with computers is as varied as their activities. The greatest amount of time is devoted to playing games, with the result that names like Nintendo have become household words. They use computers to write, to draw, to communicate, to obtain information. Some use computers as a means to establish social ties, while others use them to isolate themselves. In many cases their zeal has such force that it brings the word *addiction* to the minds of concerned parents.

The love affair involves more than the desire to do things with computers. It also has an element of possessiveness and, most importantly, of assertion of intellectual identity. Large numbers of children see the computer as "theirs"—as something that belongs to them, to their generation. Many have observed that they are more comfortable with the machines than their parents and teachers are. They learn to use them more easily and naturally. For the moment some of us old fogeys may somehow have acquired the special knowledge that makes one a master of the computer, but children know that it is just a matter of time before they inherit the machines. They are the computer generation.

What lies behind the love affair? Where is it going?

Can it be guided by the older generation into forms constructive or destructive? Or is its evolution already out of our hands?

This book focuses on one aspect of these questions: How does the relationship between children and computers affect learning? Understanding this relationship will be crucial to our ability to shape the future.

Acknowledgments

• • •

WHILE writing this book, I had many rich conversations with Mitchel Resnick, Brian Silverman, and Carol Sperry; a far smaller number with Alan Kay and Sherry Turkle; two with Paulo Freire; and none with Jean Piaget. But all these people were constantly with me as internalized voices in a virtual dialogue. Their ideas, visions, and sensibilities form the frame on which I have built this book.

Its style, which is more like a collection of finger exercises for the imagination than a scholarly treatise, does not lend itself to attributing particular ideas to specific sources. It is too allusive. Therefore, I have had to fall back on general, though deeply felt, expressions of intellectual debt to groups of people. Of these, the most important are my present and past graduate students and the Logo community at home and abroad.

I use anecdotes from classrooms the way biblical writers used parables: Stories express ideas better than any abstract statement, but the literal truth of the episodes is of secondary importance. All the incidents I recount in the book did take place as described, except that I have sometimes allowed myself license to guess what might have been in the minds of participants, and occasionally to merge several individuals into a compound character. I hope that those who recognize themselves thus partially represented will understand the spirit of respect that lies behind my expository style.

This book and all my work has gained enormously from the opportunity to work in the MIT Media Lab, whose creation by Nicholas Negroponte is an original and significant experiment in nurturing an embryonic discipline by inventing the relationships between academia and industry in which it will flourish. The lab's policies have allowed me to work with a number of commercial companies—notably Lego, Apple, IBM, Nintendo, and Logo Computer Systems—without ever feeling pressure to compromise intellectual integrity. This book, and my thinking in general, owes much more than financial support to this collaboration: In the modern world it is necessary to think of educational change as involving all sectors of society. I also owe more than financial support to the National Science Foundation, largely because Andrew Molnar has bravely managed through bad years as well as good to keep a spark of belief in change burning there.

It would be hard to capture in a few words the contribution of my editor, Susan Rabiner, to this book. If the final text is flawed, it is mostly because I outwitted her in making last-minute changes behind her back.

As a charismatic writer herself, my wife, Suzanne Massie, knew unerringly when I was on a good track and when I was not. As a superbly competent professional editor, she often spent hours cutting and pasting pages I thought were hopeless until I saw a shape emerge, like a sculpture from a rock. She exercised extraordinary ingenuity, patience, and self-denial to give me the best possible conditions for work. Her presence in those aspects of life—intellectual, spiritual, and emotional—that go beyond the professional and practical is so far beyond words that I must fall silent.

The Children's Machine

1

• • •

Yearners and
Schoolers

IMAGINE a party of time travelers from an earlier century,
among them one group of surgeons and another of school-
teachers, each group eager to see how much things have
changed in their profession a hundred or more years into the
future. Imagine the bewilderment of the surgeons finding themselves in the operating room of a modern hospital. Although they
would know that an operation of some sort was being performed,
and might even be able to guess at the target organ, they would
in almost all cases be unable to figure out what the surgeon was
trying to accomplish or what was the purpose of the many strange
devices he and the surgical staff were employing. The rituals of
antisepsis and anesthesia, the beeping electronics, and even the
bright lights, all so familiar to television audiences, would be
utterly unfamiliar to them.

The time-traveling teachers would respond very differently to a
modern elementary school classroom. They might be puzzled by
a few strange objects. They might notice that some standard techniques had changed—and would likely disagree among themselves about whether the changes they saw were for the better or
the worse—but they would fully see the point of most of what

was being attempted and could quite easily take over the class. I use this parable to provide a rough-and-ready measure of the unevenness of progress across the broad front of historical change. In the wake of the startling growth of science and technology in our recent past, some areas of human activity have undergone megachange. Telecommunications, entertainment, and transportation, as well as medicine, are among them. School is a notable example of an area that has not. One cannot say that there has been no change at all in the way we dish out education to our students. Of course there has; the parable gives me a way of pointing out what most of us know about our system of schooling: Yes, it has changed, but not in ways that have substantially altered its nature. The parable sets up the question: Why, through a period when so much human activity has been revolutionized, have we not seen comparable change in the way we help our children learn?

I have posed this question in situations ranging from casual conversation to formal seminars, and with audiences ranging from children who have had only a few years of contact with School to professional educators who have spent a lifetime in it. Although the answers I have received are as varied as the expected range of responses to a Rorschach inkblot test, the distribution is far from even from one extreme to the other. Most fall on one side or the other of a great divide.

People on one side, the Schoolers, are taken aback by my question, surprised that I seem to be looking for megachange. They acknowledge that School has problems (who doesn't today?) and are very concerned about solving them. But megachange? What can you possibly mean?

Many become indignant. Talking about megachange feels to them like fiddling while Rome burns. Education today is faced with immediate, urgent problems. Tell us how to use your computers to solve some of the many immediate practical problems we have, they say.

On the other side of the great divide are the Yearners, who

respond by citing impediments to change in education such as cost, politics, the immense power of the vested interests of school bureaucrats, or the lack of scientific research on new forms of learning. These people do not say, "I can't imagine what you could possibly be looking for," because they have themselves felt the yearning for something different.

Many individual Yearners—from parents to teachers to administrators—simply find ways to get around School, particularly when they find School's problems directly constraining their aspirations for their own children. Some parents keep their children at home: There are several hundred thousand home-schoolers in the United States. Others actively seek out alternative schools or even help to create schools that offer such alternatives.

Another important class of Yearners operates as a sort of fifth column within School itself: Large numbers of teachers manage to create within the walls of their own classrooms oases of learning profoundly at odds with the education philosophy publicly espoused by their administrators; some public school districts, perhaps those where Yearners have moved into administration, have made space for Yearners within School by allowing for the establishment of alternative programs within the School system, allowing such programs to deviate from district policies on method and curriculum.

But despite the many manifestations of a widespread desire for something different, the education establishment, including most of its research community, remains largely committed to the educational philosophy of the late nineteenth and early twentieth centuries, and so far none of those who challenge these hallowed traditions has been able to loosen the hold of the educational establishment on how children are taught.

The time-traveling teachers of my parable who saw nothing in the modern classroom they did not recognize would have found many surprises had they simply gone home with one or two of the students. For there they would have found that with an industriousness and eagerness that School can seldom generate, many of the students had become intensely involved in learning the rules and strategies of what appeared at first glance to be a process much more demanding than any homework assignment. The students would define the subject as video games and what they were doing as play.

While the technology itself might first catch the eye of our visitors, they would in time, being teachers, be struck by the level of intellectual effort that the children were putting into this activity and the level of learning that was taking place, a level that seemed far beyond that which had taken place just a few hours earlier in school. The most open and honest of our time-traveling teachers might well observe that never before had they seen so much being learned in such a confined space and in so short a time.

School would have parents—who honestly don't know how to interpret their children's obvious love affair with video games—believe that children love them and dislike homework because the first is easy and the second hard. In reality, the reverse is more often true. Any adult who thinks these games are easy need only sit down and try to master one. Most are hard, with complex information—as well as techniques—to be mastered, the information often much more difficult and time consuming to master than the technique.

If that argument did not convince parents that the games are not serious, surely a second argument would: Video games are toys—electronic toys, no doubt, but toys—and of course children like toys better than homework. By definition, play is entertaining, homework is not. What some parents may not realize, however, is that video games, being the first example of computer technology applied to toy making, have nonetheless been the entryway for children into the world of computers. These toys, by empowering children to test out ideas about working within pre-fixed rules and structures in a way few other toys are capable of doing, have proved capable of teaching students about the possibilities and drawbacks of a newly presented system in ways many adults should envy.

Video games teach children what computers are beginning to teach adults—that some forms of learning are fast-paced, immensely compelling, and rewarding. The fact that they are enormously demanding of one's time and require new ways of thinking remains a small price to pay (and is perhaps even an advantage) to be vaulted into the future. Not surprisingly, by comparison School strikes many young people as slow, boring, and frankly out of touch.

The introduction of computers is not the first challenge to education values. For example, John Dewey began his campaign for a more active and self-directed style of learning in schools over a hundred years ago, and in these intervening years numerous more or less radical reformers have strived to change School. Back then Dewey undertook his formidable task armed with little more than a strong philosophical sense about the way children develop, for at the time there was no strong movement from society in general for change in schools. There was certainly no dissatisfaction with education in Dewey's time as strong as the current one, which seems at times willing to accept the virtual destruction of the public school system rather than have things continue as they now are. Dewey remains a hero to those who believe in a twentieth-century vision of a child as a person with the right to intellectual self-determination, and there can be little doubt that a child treated with respect and encouragement rather than threatened with rejection and punishment will fare better under any system of education. But while Dewey's influence has surely removed some of the cruelest impediments to the healthy development of the child, it has been so diluted that it barely addresses the next serious question: In trying to teach children what adults want them to know, does School utilize the way human beings most naturally learn in nonschool settings?

The failure of past reformers to bring about dramatically better learning has armed those within the educational establishment with the argument that future proposals will prove no more capable of bringing about radically improved learning. Some may well believe that the best argument against megachange is this: If it has so long been so desperately needed, why have previous calls for it not caught fire? But the establishment may be in for a shock. This book is informed and shaped by the belief that strong feelings of dissatisfaction within society at large are rapidly making it impossible to save education as we know it by continuing to tinker around at its edges. Not the least of these dissatisfactions are the feelings of children. In the past, children may not have liked School, but they were persuaded to believe that it was the passport to success in life. To the extent that children reject School as out of touch with contemporary life, they become active agents in creating pressure for change. Like any other social structure, School needs to be accepted by its participants. It will not survive very long beyond the time when children can no longer be persuaded to accord it a degree of legitimation.

With much more persuasive power than the philosophy of even so radical a thinker as Dewey, the computer, in all its various manifestations, is offering the Yearners new opportunities to craft alternatives. The only question that remains is, Will such alternatives be created democratically? Will public education lead the way or, as in most things, will the change first enhance the lives of the children of the wealthy and powerful and only slowly and with much effort find its way into the lives of the children of the rest of us? Will School continue to impose a single way of knowing on everyone, or will it adapt to an epistemological pluralism? Because I am committed to democratic choice, much of this book will be devoted to looking at samples of what Yearners have done with the few opportunities they have had for bringing about change in public elementary schools. Most of the examples I use will be realistically modest in scale. They are offered not as exact pictures of the future but rather as an intimation of the rich potential that the future might hold. The following story, part fact and part fantasy, will help illustrate where I hope to go with this book.

The factual part involves an encounter I had with a four-year-old preschooler. Jennifer heard that I had grown up in Africa and asked me whether I knew how giraffes sleep. "They have such long necks," she said, and wondered where they put their heads when they rest. I said (truthfully) that I didn't know, and asked what she thought. She explained her problem with a gesture of cozying her head in folded arms: "My dog cuddles her head when she sleeps and so do I, but the giraffe's head is so far away." I pursued the conversation with other children who joined us, and gleaned a bumper crop of good theories. One suggested that the giraffe sleeps standing up "like a horse." This set off an animated discussion, which kept coming back to the question of where the animal puts its head. No one offered that the head might stay up high. Someone said it can put its head on the ground if it does a split. Jennifer, who had moved over to the idea of their sleeping standing up, showed obvious delight when she hit on a theory: "It finds a tree with a branch for its neck." I asked what would happen if there were no tree. She looked at me disdainfully and informed me that of course there would be trees—giraffes eat the tops of trees, that's why they have such long necks.

In this conversation we see two sides of the intellectual life of children of this age: the coexistence of a remarkable capacity for making theories with a nearly helpless dependence on adults for information that will test the theories or otherwise bring them into contact with reality. Jennifer is in a stage of transition. Younger children are more completely engrossed by a world within the range of immediate exploration. At a later age, unless, as too often happens, the spirit of inquiry has been extinguished, they will be able to explore a world beyond touch and sight.

Back in my own home that evening, still stimulated by my talk with the children, I threw myself into an exploration of giraffes with the intensity and perhaps even the immediacy of Jennifer's interactions with her puppy. I do not keep a pet giraffe, but I do have a library of books, of which quite a few were soon strewn all over my work area as I continued, with diversions en route, a rewarding chase after information about the sleep habits of giraffes. I was able to explore this world because the books gave me an extended immediacy.

Until recently it would have sounded silly to ask why this extended immediacy could not be available to Jennifer. Children her age cannot read, or even if they can they would not be able to conduct that kind of search. But this answer is no longer convincing. No technical obstacle stands in the way of making a machine—let's call it the Knowledge Machine—that would put the power to know what others know into Jennifer's hands. It is almost twenty years since my MIT colleague Nicholas Negroponte built a machine that allowed the vicarious exploration of the small town of Aspen, Colorado, through a computer. Extremely primitive examples are now trickling into commercial production under names like "interactive video" or electronic book, "ebook" or "CDI," or, in slightly more elaborate versions, "virtual reality."

What separates these endeavors from a true Knowledge Machine is no longer a lack of storage or access technology but the size of the effort needed to bring together the knowledge. But the enormous potential market for a Knowledge Machine makes its eventual appearance inevitable.

Such a system would enable a Jennifer of the future to explore a world significantly richer than what I was offered by my printed books. Using speech, touch, or gestures, she would steer the machine to the topic of interest, quickly navigating through a knowledge space much broader than the contents of any printed encyclopedia. Whether she is interested in giraffes or panthers or fleas, whether she wants to see them eating, sleeping, walking, running, jumping, fighting, birthing, or copulating, she would be able to find her way to the relevant sounds and images she believes would help her understand what she wants to understand. Though nothing in my argument here depends on it, this availability will one day be extended to experiencing the very smell and touch and maybe the kinesthesia of being with the animals.

The Knowledge Machine so described barely scratches the surface of how new media will change children's relationships with knowledge. But even the most superficial consideration of this question requires one elemental but consequential concession: Children who grow up with the opportunity to explore the jungles and the cities and the deep oceans and ancient myths and outer space will be even less likely than the players of video games to sit quietly through anything even vaguely resembling the elementary-school curriculum as we have known it up to now!

A less superficial consideration leads one to ask: How would the introduction of Knowledge Machines into the School environment compromise the primacy with which we view reading and writing—that is, children's fluency in using the alphabetic language?

In the literature on education there has long been a pervasive tendency to assume that reading is the principal access route to knowledge for students. Someone who cannot read is said to be doomed to ignorance, or at least to dependence on that limited amount of important information that can be obtained orally.

The educational development of children is therefore seen as rigidly dependent on learning to read in a timely way. The prospect of the Knowledge Machine suggests that this basic assumption may not necessarily be true for all time, and indeed may start to unravel within a decade or two. I am not suggesting that the written language is likely to be abandoned. I am suggesting that new thinking is needed about the position assigned to it as the prerequisite to the accumulation by students of useful knowledge, or at least as the first route to be opened to children when they begin their formal educations.

I have even firmer convictions about another kind of issue raised by the Knowledge Machine and the primacy of reading in our present culture as the essential route to knowledge. Learning to read and write is an important part of what is happening to Jennifer in the first grade, but it is not necessarily at the core of what is being communicated to her about what learning is all about. Jennifer's transition is really epistemic; although she is totally unaware of it, she is being shifted from reliance on one dominant way of knowing to reliance on another.

As an infant she acquired knowledge by exploration. She was

in charge of her learning. Though her parents put knowledge in her path, she chose what she would investigate, determining for herself what she would think about and how she would think about it. This is not to say that adults did not try to a lesser or greater extent to control her and her learning. But it is well documented that preschoolers do not deposit the knowledge adults try to feed them in their memory banks in the same way they learn to do later on, when they go to school. It is metabolized, assimilated with all their other direct experiences of the world.

When Jennifer asked me about the giraffe, however, she was at a stage when more questions were coming up in her mind than she could answer by direct exploration of her immediate world. She responded in a way she had been taught to respond: Ask a sympathetic adult who would reward her curiosity with praise. While pressure toward this mode of learning—by being told, by accepting authority—has its roots in a student's own curiosity, it will in the course of the educational experience of most children be massively reinforced by School. Where Jennifer will come out in the end will depend on many social, psychological, and accidental factors. What is clear is that she is entering a period of transition that will have a profound and perhaps brutal and dangerous impact on her intellectual development. Common School parlance often uses the word *literacy* to refer to the state of being able to read and write. However, thinkers who try to look more deeply into what education means have written scathingly in criticism of the idea that illiteracy can be remedied by teaching children the mechanical skill of decoding black marks on white paper. Much more is involved. Paulo Freire enjoins us not to dissociate "reading the word" from "reading the world." Becoming literate means thinking differently than one did previously, seeing the world differently, and this suggests that there are many different literacies.

In this sense, the choice of name for the process becomes epistemological; writers have more recently suggested as substitutes for this *literacy* the term *ways of knowing*. I am entirely in sympathy with the intentions of these writers but feel deprived of a word for the distinction between a literal sense of literacy and the various more sophisticated senses the idea evokes.

In desperation I have coined the words *letteracy* and *letterate* to refer to the special skill involved in reading words made up of alphabetical letters. Outside this more narrow definition will remain the opportunities, offered for the most part by the new media represented symbolically by the Knowledge Machine, allowing students to become highly literate independent of their progress toward letteracy.

The need for such linguistic maneuvers reflects the radical nature of the revolution in media introduced by the computer. Without risk of serious oversimplification one can say that there have been, up to now, two widely used media for the transmission of information and ideas and only one major historical transition.

For most of human history speech stood alone as the transmitter of what had previously been learned. Drawings, smoke signals, and gestures were important supplements to speech but never threatened the monopoly of speech in determining what information people in any society would share, group to group or even generation to generation. Writing was the first significant departure from the oral tradition, and whether the emergence of written language dates back to Egyptian hieroglyphics or Gutenberg is a matter of detail.

Filmmakers, painters, and other users of evolving media may be slighted by my decision to count computer-based media as the next substantive advance. But I think that Jennifer's story captures better than abstract words an important aspect of what makes the new media qualitatively different. It especially makes clear by showing us an alternative to the risk children are placed in by the fact that literacy and letteracy are virtually synonymous. They are at risk because they do not have access to a wider immediacy for exploration and have only very limited sources to which they can address questions. They are doubly at risk because the situation consolidates School in its traditional role of imposing letteracy and all the rigidity that goes with that role.

It is not surprising, given the newness of this technology, that we have developed no universally accepted language to use in talking about it. But this does not mean that we should be unaware that a revolution is in the making, or that we should not do everything possible to guide its development. For in regard to the questions of how to reform elementary education, the movement from letteracy to media-based knowledge acquisition may be even more important than the movement from preletterate to letterate culture.

It is important to remember that the letteracy revolution (that is to say, the advent of writing and printing) did not directly touch the primary ways in which most two- or four- or even six-year-olds explore the world and learn about it. Of course, the really big questions about the future of literacy and letteracy are beyond the scope of this book. But what is important here is that the Knowledge Machine offers children a transition between preschool learning and true literacy in a way that is more personal, more negotiational, more gradual, and so less precarious than the abrupt transition we now ask children to make as they move from learning through direct experience to using the printed word as the source of important information.

Why, then, would anyone fail to take seriously, as Schoolers do, something that could be so consequential for the educational process? Willfulness? A stubborn refusal to abandon old ways? These factors are present in any challenge to long-established procedures. The problem in education has an additional element. Most honest Schoolers are locked into the assumption that School's way is the only way because they have never seen or imagined convincing alternatives in the ability to impart certain kinds of knowledge.

Even the most confirmed Schooler will readily concede that some important learning happens very successfully under conditions very different from School: Babies learn to talk without curriculum or formal lessons; people develop skill at hobbies without teachers; social behavior is picked up other than through classroom instruction. A Schooler might grant that a Knowledge Machine could extend the scope of such learning to include far-away giraffes as well as nearby puppies, but still be worried by not having heard of anyone, except perhaps some highly gifted exceptions, who managed to become learned in such difficult disciplines as geometry or algebra through other than well-established and time-tested educational programs of instruction.

These skeptics have no trouble imagining, for example, a teacher leading a class of students by "Socratic questions" to "discover for themselves" some formula in mathematics. But they don't see this as significantly different than a good explanation of the formula. I have to agree with them. Although I have always yearned for ways of learning in which children act as creators rather than consumers of knowledge, the methods that have been proposed have always seemed to me marginally superior, if at all, to the old ways.

A turning point came for me in the early 1960s, when computers changed the fabric of my own work. What struck me most forcibly was that certain problems that had been abstract and hard to grasp became concrete and transparent, and certain projects that had seemed interesting but too complex to undertake became manageable. At the same time I had my first experience of the excitement and the holding power that keeps people working all night with their computers. I realized that children might be able to enjoy the same advantages—a thought that changed my life.

My goal became to strive to create an environment in which all children—whatever their culture, gender, or personality—could learn algebra and geometry and spelling and history in ways more like the informal learning of the unschooled toddler or the exceptional child than the educational process followed in schools. Stated in the language of the skeptical Schooler, my driving question was whether "exceptional children" learned differently because they were exceptional or whether, as I suspected, they became exceptional because circumstances allowed them to learn differently.

I can hear many Schoolers saying to themselves as they read this: "Yes, yes, we've heard that before. It's the old refrain of progressive education. That's been tried and it didn't work. You yourself have just poked fun at the discovery method in algebra."

There is a family resemblance (and I shall accept the word *progressive* to name it) between the vision of learning I am presenting here and certain philosophical principles expressed in the diverse forms of innovations that go under such names as *progressive* or *open* or *child-centered* or *constructivist* or *radical* education. I certainly share with this broad movement the criticism of School as casting the child in the role of passive recipient of knowledge. Paulo Freire expresses the criticism most vividly in his description of School as following a "banking model" in which information is deposited in the child's mind like money in a savings account. Other writers express the same thought by accusing School of treating the child's mind as a "vessel to be filled" or as the receiver at the end of a transmission line.

One way in which I am at variance with progressive education becomes apparent when we turn from criticizing School to inventing new methods. In my view almost all experiments purporting to implement progressive education have been disappointing because they simply did not go far enough in making the student the subject of the process rather than the object. In some cases this came about because the experimenters were too timid; the experiments failed just as the test of any medical treatment would fail if the treating doctors were afraid to give the drugs in effective dosages.

In most cases there were reasons deeper than timidity in holding them back. Early designers of experiments in progressive education lacked the *tools* that would allow them to create new methods in a reliable and systematic fashion. With very limited means at their disposal, they were forced to rely too heavily on the specific talents of individual teachers or a specific match with a particular social context. As a result, what successes they had often could not be generalized.

Another parable will emphasize this point and also clarify where I see my main new contribution to the old debate. My hypothetical Schoolers said that progressive education has been tried and did not work. I agree that it hasn't worked very well— but in something like the sense in which Leonardo da Vinci failed in his attempts to invent an airplane. Making an airplane in Leonardo's time needed more than a creative manipulation of all that was known about aeronautics. His failure to make a workable airplane did not prove him wrong in his assumptions about the feasibility of flying machines.

Leonardo's airplane had to wait for the development of something that could come about only through great changes in the way society managed its resources. The Wright Brothers could succeed where Leonardo could only dream because a technological infrastructure supplied materials and tools and engines and fuels, while a scientific culture (which developed in coevolution with this infrastructure) supplied ideas that drew on the peculiar capabilities of these new resources.

Educational innovators even in the very recent past were in a situation analogous to Leonardo's. They could and did formulate bold perspectives: for example, John Dewey's idea that children would learn better if learning were truly a part of living experience; or Freire's idea that they would learn better if they were truly in charge of their own learning processes; or Jean Piaget's idea that intelligence emerges from an evolutionary process in which many factors must have time to find their equilibrium; or Lev Vygotsky's idea that conversation plays a crucial role in learning. Such ideas have always appealed to Yearners; they resonate with a respectful attitude toward children and a democratic social philosophy.

Sadly, in practice they just wouldn't fly. When educators tried to craft an actual school based on these general principles, it was as if Leonardo had tried to make an airplane out of oak and power it with a mule. Most practitioners who tried to follow the seminal thinkers in education were forced to compromise so deeply that the original intent was lost. For example, the "discovery method" may take a step in the direction of Dewey's dream, but it is a minuscule step, utterly insufficient to make the kind of difference expressed in the grand vision of empowered children learning through living experience. It is simply double-talk to ask children to take charge of their own learning and at the same time order them to "discover" something that can have no role in helping them understand anything they care about or are interested in or curious about.

As a mode of access to knowledge of the kind Jennifer was seeking, the machine will not be more than a suggestive metaphor for some time yet to come because the quantity of factual knowledge needed to make it work is so vast. But there are other areas of knowledge where the epistemic transition is even more brutal for many children, and where a machine that will provide a context for softening it is very much closer at hand. One such area is mathematics.

If the idea of a transition from oral to letterate ways of knowing seems less applicable to mathematics, this is largely because our culture is inclined to reserve the name *mathematics* for the letterate kind of mathematics taught in school and perhaps a minimal intuitive basis directly connected with it. But by closing off a much larger basis of knowledge that should serve as a foundation for formal mathematics, we have cut off the route to better learning. Every preschool child has amassed on his or her own special mathematical knowledge about quantities, about space, about the reliability of various reasoning processes, elements that will be useful later in the math class. The enormous quantity of this "oral" mathematics constructed and retained by every child has been well documented by Jean Piaget.

The central problem for math education is to find ways to draw on the child's vast experience of oral mathematics. Computers can do this.

The most powerful use made of computers in changing the epistemological structure of children's learning to date has been the construction of microworlds, in which children pursue mathematical activity because the world into which they are drawn requires that they develop particular mathematical skills. Simultaneously, these worlds match in form the successful oral style of young children's learning. Giving children the opportunity to learn and use mathematics in a nonformalized way of knowing encourages rather than inhibits the eventual adoption of a formalized way as well, just as the Knowledge Machine, rather than discouraging reading, would eventually stimulate children to read.

In saying this I must emphasize a difference with many trends in the use of concrete or constructivist methods to teach math. The entire point of the Knowledge Machine would be lost if it were conceived solely as a device for teaching children to read. Similarly, the point of developing nonformalized ways of knowing in mathematics is entirely subverted if these are conceived as a scaffolding for learning the formal way or as a trick to lure children into formalized instruction. They have to be valued for themselves and genuinely useful to the learner in and of themselves. Many more examples of this distinction will be found in later chapters.

Here I make the point simply by looking at the original design on the next page that was made (in magnificent color, which unfortunately cannot be reproduced here) by children in a New York City middle school as part of a study of African textiles. The design was made by programming a computer in the programming language Logo using a nonformalized version of a kind of mathematics called turtle geometry. These students did not use the design process in order to learn more formal geometry. They used a kind of geometry that matched their preferred way of knowing in order to pursue ideas about African design. Geometry is not there for being learned. It is there for being used. The main exception I would make is a big one: Both geometry and learning it can be objects of love, in which case use might fall by the wayside.

The African textiles design. The drawing at right was also generated by children, using Logo to program computers in the classroom.

These remarks about formal and other geometries might be offensive to many Yearners as well as to most Schoolers. For I seem to be saying that some students should be satisfied with a kind of useful geometry other than the real McCoy, and this might be read as if it had an undertone of elitism. What I am really saying, and will develop particularly in chapter 9, is that there is room for much rethinking about what knowledge, and what ways of knowing, should have a privileged status. Certainly School has not earned the right to decide for us. Those Yearners who yearn for better ways to teach what School has decreed everyone should know have not quite accepted the idea of megachange. I hope, after reading this book, they will have moved toward questioning not only how School teaches but what as well.

A bigger departure from the curriculum is shown by a project in which children invent and build artificial creatures using a version of Lego extended to include tiny computers, which take in information from sensors and control motors. The computer can be programmed in Logo to make the creatures move in a "purposeful" way. For example, an eight-year-old girl constructed a model "mother cat" and its "kitten." Both would roam until the kitten beeped and flashed a light mounted on its head; at this signal the cat would begin to move toward it. Other children have built snakes and monsters. One team built an "intelligent" model house that cleaned itself.

The idea of programming such behavior might sound difficult. In fact, the latest user-friendly versions of Logo (such as *Microworlds Logo*) make it so easy that technological construction and the underlying scientific principles become as natural a medium for the expression of fantasy as for drawing or speech. Thus one of the subject lines that splits School's epistemology is blurred: Traditionally in School, the art and writing classes might have time for fantasy, but science deals with facts. No wonder many children find it cold. A second subject line is blurred by the union of technology with biology. Making an artificial animal is no substitute for studying real ones, but it does provide insight into aspects of real animals, for example, the principle of "feedback" that enables the Lego cat to find its kitten. The situation is analogous to the way in which the principle of lift lies behind the flight of birds and airplanes, but there is a big difference in the social importance of the two cases. While it does not matter very much whether people understand lift, feedback is a key concept for thinking about systems. The lack of ability to think fluently about the environment, the economy, or even one's family as a system matters very much indeed.

The concept of feedback illustrates how artificial it is to confine science to the precisely stated kind of knowledge favored by letteracy. The Lego cat never "knows" at all precisely where the light is located; all it "knows" is vaguely whether it is more to the left or more to the right. The program makes the cat turn a little in the appropriate direction, move a little forward, and repeat the cycle; turning one degree or ten degrees on each round will work equally well. Thus, what the cat "knows" is more in tune with the qualitative knowledge of a preletterate child than with anything precise and quantitative. The fact that it can nevertheless find its way to the exact destination is empowering for all qualitative thinkers and especially for children. It allows them to enter science through a region where scientific thinking is most like their own thinking.

The idea that partial and qualitative knowledge can be good knowledge is applicable to a discussion of whether building a Lego model is really relevant to the scientific study of biology. If one rejects all inexact knowledge, one might believe that the only way a model can elucidate nature is by simulating it precisely. The model cat shows a different kind of simulation, a "soft simulation" that provides qualitative understanding of a complex system by constructing a simple one with which it shares a principle.

The computer graphics and the artificial creature projects give a glimpse of directions of change for School that move toward megachange. The rest of this book is structured by three themes that bear on the likelihood of School actually doing so. The most down-to-earth of the three is a look at what is happening in schools. In chapter 3 I look at the response of School as an institution to the images of change I have anticipated here. Chapter 4 discusses teachers and chapter 10 discusses issues of strategy for change. The next theme is directed at developing a better sense of the evolution of the technology itself and the ideas and cultures that have come with it. This discussion permeates the entire book but is specifically focused in chapters 8 and 9. The final theme is the most controversial. I believe that if we are to have new forms of learning, we need a very different kind of theory of learning. The theories that have been developed by educational psychologists, and by academic psychologists in general, are matched to a specific kind of learning, School's kind. As long as these ways of thinking about learning remain dominant, it will be very hard to make a serious shift from the traditional form of School.

In the next chapter I give a first view of the direction in which I would look in order to find new ways of thinking. In its briefest description, this direction is within ourselves. In chapter 5 I propose giving a name to a new kind of theory of learning which will reflect the fact that human experience gives all of us a vaster store of knowledge about learning than has been accumulated by all the white-coated academics in their laboratories.

2

• • •

Personal Thinking

A course on psychology I took as an undergraduate left little residue in my mind, except for a homily on objectivity delivered in the first lecture. We were warned that many of us might have enrolled under the erroneous impression that the course, being about psychology, would provide an occasion to explore the psychological issues in our own lives. Those who had come for this reason were advised to consider whether they really wanted to be there. The starting point for the study of scientific psychology was, we were told, the skill of distancing oneself from the object of study. We would have to work hard to learn how to keep intuitions based on our own experiences out of our thinking about the psychological issues we would be studying.

Without a doubt there is a need in any discipline for skill in distancing oneself from the object of study. However, the more significant lack in the study of education is quite the opposite: There is too much distancing.

Yearners have tirelessly protested the way that School's curriculum distances knowledge from the individuality of the student. Beyond this, the quest for a science of education has led to ways of thinking about teaching that exclude the teacher as a person, and ways of thinking about education research that exclude the researcher as a person. My protest starts by situating my own work on educational innovation in my life experience.

My critique of School and yearning for something else began very early. In elementary school I already knew quite clearly that my best intellectual work was done outside the classroom. My resentment of School was mitigated only by the fact that I loved two teachers and had a handful of friends who participated with me in activities I considered to be more valuable. The most important of these was a newspaper produced by a 1930s version of desktop publishing. My printer was a homemade gelatinous block to which ink could be transferred from a glossy master sheet and thence to sheets of absorbent paper. The newspaper was important for me in many ways. Above all, it gave me a sense of identity. Adults asked one another, "What do you do?" and I could think of what I "did" as something more personal and distinctive than "going to school."

Besides this, the newspaper made connections with several areas of intellectual and social development that would shape my high school years and beyond. I developed a sense of myself and a little skill as a chemist. My printing system was initially based on an article in Arthur Mee's *Children's Encyclopedia* but evolved over time and through many experimental variations. I developed a sense of myself as a writer, and I had to shoulder financial and managerial responsibilities that were no less real for being on a very small scale. And, perhaps most important in its subsequent impact on my life, the newspaper slowly drew me into the beginnings of political activism in the highly charged atmosphere of Johannesburg, where I lived from age seven through my mid-twenties.

The particular facts of my story are unique to me as an individual; the general principles it illustrates are not. Reading biographies and interrogating friends has convinced me that all successful learners find ways to take charge of their early lives sufficiently to develop a sense of intellectual identity. A fascinating example is Jean Piaget. The case has a mild irony in that this man, so often quoted as the authority on what children cannot do because they are not at the appropriate stages of development, published his first scientific article at age eleven! What does one make of this? Devotees of Piaget often view it reverently as an early sign of his genius. In fact the short paper, which reports a sighting of a rare bird in the Swiss mountains, does not contain any logical patterns that would be surprising in an average child of eleven. I am inclined to think of the publication as being as much a cause as a consequence of Piaget's exceptional intellectual qualities, though, of course (in what he would have called a dialectical sense), it is surely both.

Piaget's article did not just happen as a consequence of some quality of his mind. He explains it as a simple intentional act. He wanted to be allowed to use the college library in his small Swiss town, and wrote and published the article to make the librarian take him seriously enough to give him permission to do so. What I find most impressive in the story is not that a boy of eleven could write a report about a bird but that this same boy of eleven took himself seriously enough to conceive and carry out this strategy for dealing with the librarian. I see in it young Jean preparing himself to become Piaget. He was practicing taking charge of his own development, something that is necessary not only for those who want to become leading thinkers but for all citizens of a society in which individuals have to define and redefine their roles throughout a long lifetime.

In stark contrast with the image of Piaget the child constructing Piaget the adult, School has an inherent tendency to infantilize children by placing them in a position of having to do as they are told, to occupy themselves with work dictated by someone else and that, moreover, has no intrinsic value—schoolwork is done only because the designer of a curriculum decided that doing the work would shape the doer into a desirable form. I find this offensive, in part because I remember how much I objected as a child to being placed in that situation, but mainly because I am convinced that the best learning takes place when the learner takes charge, as the young Piaget did. Thus my antennae are always out for initiatives that will allow the purpose of School as a place for learning to coexist with a culture of personal responsibility.

This must not be confused with the faddish idea that what children learn should be made "relevant"—so, teacher, don't just make them add numbers, pretend you are shopping in the supermarket. Children are not easily duped. If they sense that they are being made to play a silly game, they will be discouraged from taking themselves seriously. I liked a little better what I saw at the Lamplighter School in Dallas, where the fourth-grade children actually had real responsibility for operating an egg business. They bought the feed, cleaned the coops, collected and sold the eggs, and kept the profit, if there was any, at the end of the year. If they ended up with a loss, they had to explain themselves to the next class. But even this allowed very little opportunity for real initiative and only a minor sense of doing something really important.

A deeper sense of doing something important in itself is visible in the project "Kidnet," developed in a collaboration between the National Geographic Society and Robert Tinker, who is responsible for developing some of the best uses of computers for learning science. This project engages middle school students to collect data about acid rain. The individual schools send their data across electronic networks to a central computer where it is integrated and sent back to the local sites, where it can be analyzed and discussed in the context of globally important problems. The project hints at a vision of millions of children all over the world engaged in work that makes a real contribution to the scientific study of a socially urgent problem. In principle, a million children could collect more data about the environment than any socially affordable number of professional scientists.

This is infinitely better than School's ritualistic worksheets and demonstration experiments, if only because the students feel they are engaged in a meaningful and socially important activity they really care about. However, what I like most is the opportunity it offers the students to break out of its own framework to engage in more self-directed activities. One way that students break out quite frequently is to use the expertise acquired in the project to engage in local environmental campaigns. Another example that pleased me particularly was expressed by a student who had worked out a plan to bypass the use of children to collect data by automating these operations. He explained that the children could then devote themselves to more important environmental work! This student could not actually implement this plan with the means provided by his school, but he was close: In a few years such projects will use hardware and software flexible enough for this student's plan to be widely implemented.

A different example of computers giving children the opportunity to develop a sense of doing serious work is that of two fifth-grade boys with very different interests, one in science and the other in dance and music, who came together to create a "screen choreography" by programming a computer set up in the back of the classroom. What they were doing may not have been relevant, but it certainly felt vitally important to these boys and was seen as such by their teacher, who encouraged them to take time from regular class work for their project. Watching them, I was reminded of the newspaper I worked on as a child. I guessed that they were growing as independent intellectual agents, and anyone could see that they were learning what was for their age an unusual amount of mathematics and computer programming.

This discussion, which intermingles learning incidents from my life and Piaget's with incidents from the lives of children in contemporary schools, represents an alternative to the methodology favored by the dominant "scientific" school of thought. Researchers, following the so-called scientific method of using controlled experiments, solemnly expose children to a "treatment" of some sort and then look for measurable results. But this flies in the face of all common knowledge of how human beings develop. Although it is obvious to me that my newspaper played a profound role in my intellectual development, I am pretty sure that no test would have detected its role by comparing my "performance" the day before I started and three months later. The significant effects emerged over a much longer period, to be measured, probably, in years. Moreover, an experiment that gave a hundred children "the experience of producing a newspaper," even if continued for several years, still would miss the point of what happened to me. The significant engagement was too personal to be expected to operate as a mass effect; I fell in love with my newspapering (as I did with mathematics and other areas of knowledge) for reasons that are as personal and in a sense as unreproducible as those that determine any kind of falling in love.

The method of controlled experimentation that evaluates an idea by implementing it, taking care to keep everything else the same, and measuring the result, may be an appropriate way to evaluate the effects of a small modification. However, it can tell us nothing about ideas that might lead to deep change. One cannot simply implement such ideas to see whether they lead to deep change: A megachanged system can come into being only through a slow, organic evolution, and through a close harmony with social evolution. It will be steered less by the outcome of tests and measurements than by its participants' intuitive understanding.

The most powerful resource for this process is exactly what is denied by objective psychology and the would-be science of education. Every one of us has built up a stock of intuitive, empathic, commonsense knowledge about learning. This knowledge comes into play when one recognizes something good about a learning experience without knowing the outcome. It seems obvious to me that every good teacher uses this kind of knowledge far more than test scores or other objective measurements in daily decisions about students. Perhaps the most important problem in education research is how to mobilize and strengthen such knowledge.

One step toward strengthening it is to recognize it. The denial of personal intuitive knowledge has led to a profound split in thinking about learning; the split recalls the theory that each of us has two brains which think in fundamentally different ways. By analogy, one might say that when it comes to thinking about learning, nearly all of us have a School side of the brain, which thinks that School is the only natural way to learn, and a personal side that knows perfectly well it is not.

A second strategy for strengthening the personal side and breaking the stranglehold of the School side is to develop a methodology for reflection about cases of successful learning and especially about one's own best learning experiences. Analogies with two events in the history of aviation—a case of true megachange—will clarify my thinking.

People who dreamed about making flying machines looked at birds in the same spirit as I want to look at examples of successful learning. But it was not enough simply to look and copy. Many were misled into thinking that the essence of bird flight was the flapping of wings. Even the great Leonardo was drawn into the vision of an ornithopter, a machine that would look like a bird and fly by flapping birdlike wings. This was not the way to make a flying machine. Nevertheless, it was the observation of birds that provided the secret. My analogy here concerns John Wilkins, a seventeenth-century bishop, scientist, and founder of the Royal Society. Wilkins could not have been the first to observe that birds could fly without flapping their wings. But he was one of the first to see the importance in this otherwise banal observation. He was right. The simplicity of a gull soaring without a visible movement of its body became the model that eventually led to formulating the principle of lift, the concept underlying both the understanding of natural flyers and the making of artificial flyers. We have to learn to see successful learning through the prism of such powerful ideas.

The second event happened as an indirect result of the first. The year 1903—when a powered airplane first flew successfully—was a turning point in the history of transportation. But the famous flyer made by Wilbur and Orville Wright did not prove itself by its performance. The duration of the best of several flights that day was only fifty-nine seconds! As a practical alternative to the horse-drawn wagon, it was laughable. Yet imaginative minds could see in it the birth of the industry that would lead to the jumbo jet and the space shuttle. Thinking about the future of education demands a similar labor of the imagination. The prevalent literal-minded, "what you see is what you get" approach measuring the effectiveness of computers in learning by the achievements in present-day classrooms makes it certain that tomorrow will always be the prisoner of yesterday. Indeed, the situation in education is often even worse than judging the effectiveness of airplanes by the fifty-nine-second flight. It is more like attaching a jet engine to an old-fashioned wagon to see whether it will help the horses. Most probably it would frighten the animals and shake the wagon to pieces, "proving" that jet technology is actually harmful to the enhancement of transportation.

I have in my files a large collection of scientific papers reporting experiments that try to measure "the effect of computers on learning." It is like measuring the flight characteristics of the Wrights' flyer to determine "the effect of flying on transportation." The significance of the flyer could be appreciated by hard imaginative work based on understanding the principles, such as "lift," which lay behind the design. In order to find the corresponding principles for learning, we have to look into ourselves as much as at computers: Principles such as "taking charge" and "intellectual identity" and "falling in love" (as I used in talking about my newspaper) have come to play that role in my own thinking as a direct result of observing myself when I seemed to be flying intellectually. The incidents in the rest of this chapter highlight some others.

As I grew up, learning became a hobby. Of course any hobby involves learning, but most people are more interested in what they learn than in how the learning happens. In fact, most learn without giving a thought to learning. I often go to the other extreme. I learned to juggle, to fly a plane, and to cook, not only because I wanted to do these things but also because I wondered what the learning would be like. Though I came to love all these hobbies for their own sake, part of my pleasure in them has always been that of observing myself learn and making up theories about how I do so. A good example of this process is how I learned to make croissants.

When I got croissant making right after many, many failures, I allowed myself some elation but then began to worry about what had happened. One day I couldn't do it, the next day I could! What had changed? In order to reconstruct the moment of transition, I tried to recapture the state of "inability" I had been in the day before. At first I thought in terms of external factors such as the proportions of ingredients, the times of rising and resting, and the temperatures of dough, working surface, and oven. But varying these did not seem to account for my prior uneven results.

When I eventually did relive the key moment, I had learned about much more than making croissants. The difference between before and after lay in feeling the degree of "squishiness" of the butter through the squishiness of the pastry dough and through my heavy marble rolling pin. Trying to capture this deliberately seemed at first like the princess and the pea. I tried many times. It was only when I decided that I had enough and would give up for the day that a breakthrough happened. On my marble slab was a last parcel of butter wrapped in dough. Wondering what to do with it, I playfully flattened it with the rolling pin, relaxed, without trying to do anything in particular—and all of a sudden I felt distinctly the structure of the mass of matter. Once I felt it, I knew "in my fingers" how to make a croissant, and now when I try after an interval of several years, the knack always comes back by the second batch—though if I had to do it on a school test I would fail, because I need the spoiled first try to get the feel for the successful second one.

When I retell such experiences to an audience of educators, I always hope that someone will be annoyed by my talk of croissants and say: "What has this to do with grammar or math or writing business letters? Naturally in cooking you have to learn to feel the relationship of your body to matter. But math is not about feeling relationships of your body to numbers." I like this reaction because it brings out into the open something that lurks in the culture and allows me to confront it.

A few years ago I would have begun with the rejoinder: "You think that math does not have anything to do with the body because you are not a mathematician; if you were you would know that mathematics is full of gut feelings and all sorts of kinesthetics." Today I would say it the other way around: "The reason you are not a mathematician might well be that you think that math has nothing to do with the body; you have kept your body out of it because it is supposed to be abstract, or perhaps a teacher scolded you for using your fingers to add numbers!" This idea is not just metaphysics. It has inspired me to use the computer as a medium to allow children to put their bodies back into their mathematics.

My favorite example is an invention called "the turtle." You can think of this as a drawing instrument whose simplest use will become clear from the following scenario. Imagine that you are looking at a computer screen. On it you see a small turtle, which moves when you type commands in a language called "turtle talk," leaving a line as it goes. The command "Forward 50" causes the turtle to move straight ahead a certain distance. "Forward 100" will make it move in the same direction twice as far. You soon get the idea that the numbers represent the distance it moves; they can be thought of as turtle steps. Now if you want to make it go in a different direction, you give it a command like "Right 90." It stays in the same place but turns on itself, facing east if it had previously been facing north. With this knowledge you should easily be able to make it draw a square. If that's easy for you, you can think about how to draw a circle, and if that's easy, you can try a spiral. Somewhere you will meet your level of difficulty, and when you do I'll give you this piece of advice: Put yourself in the place of the turtle. Imagine yourself moving in a square or a circle or a spiral or whatever it may be. You may resist for a while because you are tense and trying too hard, as I was with my croissants. But when you let yourself go, you will find that there is a richer source of mathematical knowledge in your body than in classroom textbooks.

Learning to speak French was one of my most instructive learning experiences. Although this was not a case of learning for its own sake—I went to live in Paris to complete my doctoral research in mathematics—my professional purpose was interlaced with playful learning experiments. For example, I developed a relationship with an eight-year-old boy who was delighted to be my "professor." He was young enough to be "studying French" at the same time as I was. Although he was a native speaker, he was learning spelling and grammar at school and was acquiring vocabulary at an appreciable rate. I was able to compare the speed and pattern of my progress with his, and in doing so established a curious fact: By any measure I could think of, I was learning faster. I could have attributed the discrepancy between this observation and the common linguistic sluggishness of adults to some kind of special "gift for languages." I didn't. I explain the discrepancy by the fact that I was learning French mostly like a child but could also take advantage of some sophisticated ideas that a child would not know. On the one hand, I was open to playful immersion; on the other, I could make occasional use of formal linguistics. Somewhere between the two was the fact that my learning of French seemed to be facilitated by experimenting (or playing) not only with French but also with learning itself. Studying one's own learning process—as the example of croissant making also shows—can be a powerful method of enhancing learning. In any case, looking back I see an important root of my present ideas in this recognition of the advantages of combining childlike and adultlike ways of learning.

Although my mathematical research in Paris earned me my

Ph.D., the Parisian discovery that had the biggest impact on my life was Jean Piaget, who at the time was giving a course at the Sorbonne. I got to know him and was invited to work in his center in Geneva, where I spent the next four years and became passionately interested in children's thinking. If the key ideas in this book first crossed my mind then, however, they were in the most nebulous guise. In particular, I made no connection that I can remember between my own learning and the process of intellectual development of children on which we worked at Piaget's center. The reason is significant: We were all too serious and too formal about children's thinking. Of course we thought about their play; it was Piaget who coined the oft-quoted line that play is child's work. But no one in that environment was looking at the other half of this pithy aphorism: the idea that work (at least serious intellectual work) might be adult's play. We thought of children as "little scientists" but did not think much about the complementary idea of viewing scientists as "big children."

Following the four years in Geneva, I became a professor of mathematics at MIT. Many factors made the move attractive. There was the prospect of access to computers and of working with Marvin Minsky and Warren McCulloch, as well as a wonderful sense of playfulness that I had experienced there on brief visits. When I finally arrived, all this came together in all-night sessions around a PDP-1 computer that had been given to Minsky. It was pure play. We were finding out what could be done with a computer, and anything interesting was worthwhile. Nobody yet knew enough to decree that some things were more serious than others. We were like infants discovering the world.

It was in this situation that I thought about computers and children. I was playing like a child and experiencing a volcanic explosion of creativity. Why couldn't the computer give a child the same kind of experience? Why couldn't a child play like me? What would have to be done to make this possible?

These questions launched me on a new quest guided by the Robin Hood–like idea of stealing technology from the lords of the laboratories and giving it to the children of the world. A first step in the quest was to recognize that one of the sources of the technologists' power was the veil of esoteric mystery woven around the idea of programming. The situation is quite analogous to the way priests of other ages kept power from people by monopolizing the ability to read and write, and by keeping what they considered the most powerful knowledge in languages the common people could not understand. I saw the need to make computer languages that could be "vulgarized"—made available to ordinary people and especially children.

This has turned out to be a long and difficult task. Computer languages, like natural languages, cannot be "made"; they have to evolve. What could be made was a first shot at such a language, named Logo, which would serve as a starting point for a longer evolution that is in fact still continuing.

For the sake of concreteness, the ideas in this book are developed through the story of my own inventions. I make no secret of the fact that I love and value some of them. I believe that some may even have a long-term future. But I repeat that my purpose here is not to tell the reader how to do things right but to provoke and fuel imaginations. In this book my real-life inventions serve the same purpose as the imaginary examples of time travelers and hypothetical nineteenth-century engineers. They are meant to evoke further ideas, to prepare our minds for other, much more exciting inventions still to be made. My purpose could not be further removed from advocating a particular invention as *the* solution to *the* problem of education; rather, each example is meant to serve as a pointer to a vast area of new opportunities for educational invention. My goal in relation to Schoolers—or to anyone who thinks that any form of learning is the right and natural form of learning—is to stir the imagination to invent alternatives. Piaget said that to understand is to invent. He was thinking of children. But the principle applies to all of us.

3

• • •

School: Change and Resistance to Change

I made a first pass at creating images of educational mega-change in *Mindstorms: Children, Computers, and Powerful Ideas*, written in the late 1970s, a time when personal computers were still novelties. IBM had not yet moved into the field, nor had the Japanese. The original Apple was mostly the darling of enthusiastic computer hobbyists.

The subtitle of the book reflects a gap in my experience and knowledge by mentioning children and excluding school. Children's involvement with computers had already begun. The first primitive video games had appeared, and one could mount experiments in which large and expensive machines simulated the still nonexistent personal computer. Children's interest in what they could do with the machines was not distracted by knowing that a million-dollar machine stood behind the terminal used in the experimental setting. No similar experiment could be done on what schools might do in a world in which computers would be everyday objects. Their reaction was so profoundly determined by considerations of price and size that no "simulation" could provide insights into how they would allocate real budget and accept real changes in their organization. It is not surprising, then, that my discussion of schools lacked the texture that real experience gave to the discussion of how computers could mediate between children and ideas. I was not the only one to suffer from this failing; in fact, a persistent tunnel vision continues to deform public discussion of the relationship between technology and schools. My purpose in this chapter is to develop a wider-angled view.

Mindstorms was written at a turning point in the development of educational computing. At that time, there were at most a handful of classrooms in which anything like the classroom incidents mentioned in the previous chapter could possibly have taken place; in fact, the only activities in the field that I know of were two formal research projects, my own and a related one mounted by Alan Kay, a seminal contributor to the idea that the computer could be an instrument for everyone. Yet two years after the book was published, there were hundreds of classrooms in which one could see similar events, and two years later still, there were tens of thousands. This growth of a school computer culture was still far from megachange, but it had reached proportions that made it incomparably richer as a source of insight into educational change than the cramped experiments of the previous decade. In ten years American schools had bought three million computers; tens of thousands of teachers enrolled in classes to learn about computers; new industrial giants moved into the education market; twenty thousand items purporting to be "educational software" were offered for sale.

These dramatic events did not fail to attract media attention. Apart from the sheer numbers, the very idea of a small child using a computer gave people a sense that something new, exciting, and a little disturbing was in the air. Add to this the photogenic quality of children with eyes made brighter by the light of the screen, and it is understandable that computers in schools for a while aroused more enthusiastic coverage in the press than sensible discussion about what it all meant. But what did it mean? What sensible questions would lead to understanding what was happening and where it might go? A headline in the *Wall Street Journal* reflected the doubts of sensible people interested in the bottom line. SCHOOLS BUY MANY COMPUTERS, it proclaimed, BUT BENEFITS IN CLASS-ROOMS ARE SMALL. The tone of skepticism is understandable. Talk of crisis in the schools was on the rise. Even in the uncritical climate of Reagan's Washington, the report "A Nation at Risk" had dramatically proclaimed this. It is not surprising that questions were asked: Where are all those computers we have heard so much about? What are they doing? Far from producing improvement, they seemed unable even to stop the deterioration.

I offer two replies to the kind of doubts raised by the *Journal,* one relatively superficial and one more serious. The superficial response concerns the use of the word *many* to describe the number of computers in the schools, which at the time was between one and two million. Was this a lot? Yes, if one thought of a mountain of computers piled up in one's backyard. No, if one divided it by the number of students in all those classrooms. I know what it is like to have had my intellectual life change, and more than once, through using computers. In addition to intellectually deeper changes, my writing habits have changed because I take a computer on a plane, in a car, out on the lawn, or to the bathroom; and my communication habits have changed as a consequence of so many colleagues and friends being in touch through electronic mail. Just two days ago I clarified my thinking about the economic reform in Russia by programming a soft simulation of economic competition. This can happen because I have a computer, in fact several computers, within reach at most times.

The critical level at which computers really make a difference is surely less than what I have, but equally surely more than what schools offer most students. A million computers divided among fifty million students gives each of them one-fiftieth of a computer. I do not think that the significant benefits that computers have brought me would have accrued from a fiftieth of a machine. Simple arithmetic, which is not altered in principle by the fact that some schools may have had three or four times the average number of computers, provides so obvious an explanation of the *Journal*'s puzzle that one wonders whether the journalists who wrote the article were really thinking in any concrete sense about what they were writing. I wonder whether they would be surprised if observation of schools in some country where only one writing instrument could be provided for every fifty students suggested that writing does not significantly help learning.

The argument that a small number of computers is unlikely to produce big change might seem to be contradicted by some of the incidents mentioned earlier, where children enjoyed the experience of sharing two computers with a whole class. There is no doubt that, with or without computers, an isolated event can sometimes precipitate important intellectual growth. But more often, change requires a much longer and more social computer experience than is possible with two machines at the back of a classroom. In chapter 6 we'll meet Debbie, who did have an "aha" experience about the meaning of mathematics, but she was in a school which owned over a hundred computers. Also, such change is often reversible, as in the case of Raymond, whose experience with computers gave him his first taste of enjoyable and successful learning at school. This student who had been classified as "learning disabled" produced a quality of work that astonished his teachers, his parents, and even himself. However, this taste of something better aggravated his dislike of the ways of regular classroom life to such an extent that in the end he rejected school even more deeply than he had before his computer experience.

Another reason for small effect involves deeper problems than that of numbers. In the early 1980s there were few microcomputers in schools, but those few were almost all in the classrooms of visionary teachers, most of whom employed them in a "progressive" spirit, cutting across School's practices of balkanized curriculum and impersonal rote learning. Thereafter, however, the pattern changed sharply. The initiative and the power in the field of computers were moving from teachers to school administrations—most often at the city or even at the state level. When there were few computers in the school, the administration was content to leave them in the classrooms of teachers who showed greatest enthusiasm, and these were generally teachers who were excited about the computer as an instrument of change. But as the numbers grew and computers became something of a status symbol, the administration moved in. From an administrator's point of view, it made more sense to put the computers together in one room—misleadingly named "computer lab"—under the control of a specialized computer teacher. Now all the children could come together and study computers for an hour a week. By an inexorable logic the next step was to introduce a curriculum for the computer. Thus, little by little the subversive features of the computer were eroded away: Instead of cutting across and so challenging the very idea of subject boundaries, the computer now defined a new subject; instead of changing the emphasis from impersonal curriculum to excited live exploration by students, the computer was now used to reinforce School's ways. What had started as a subversive instrument of change was neutralized by the system and converted into an instrument of consolidation.

This analysis directly contradicts the answer most commonly given by researchers when asked why computers have made so little dent in the problems faced by School. They are inclined to say that "schools don't know how to use the computer"; and they propose to remedy this by more research on methods of using computers, by developing more software, especially software that will be easier to use, and by setting up channels of dissemination of knowledge about computers. They are fundamentally wrong. Of course, research will increase the variety and effectiveness of uses of computers, but this is not what will change the nature of computer use in schools. The shift from a radically subversive instrument in the classroom to a blunted conservative instrument in the computer lab came neither from a lack of knowledge nor from a lack of software. I explain it by an innate intelligence of

School, which acted like any living organism in defending itself against a foreign body. It put into motion an immune reaction whose end result would be to digest and assimilate the intruder. Progressive teachers knew very well how to use the computer for their own ends as an instrument of change; School knew very well how to nip this subversion in the bud. No one in the story acted out of ignorance about computers, although they might have been naïve in failing to understand the sociological drama in which they were actors.

This view of the development of computers in schools points to a very different approach to what can be learned from the experience of computers in schools than that of the *Wall Street Journal* article. The question has shifted from "Did it succeed, yes or no?" to "What actually took place below the surface; what can we learn from the experience that will inform future strategies?" The principal "lesson" I learned represents a significant shift from the views I advanced in *Mindstorms,* and what is still customary in the field of educational computing.

The shift is analogous to the emergence of developmental teaching, which eschews molding a mind as if it were a passive medium and instead tries to collaborate with the student's developmental patterns. If the student does not progress in the expected way, the developmental teacher tries to understand what happened, rather than branding the student as a failure. Looking below the surface one can often see an inner coherence in what appeared to be just plain wrong, one sees mental roadblocks that stand in the way of progress, and one sees dynamic elements that can be mobilized to serve it. *Mindstorms'* ideas about children were quite thoroughly developmental, but I now blush at recognizing how my thinking about School contravened basic developmental canons. I characterized much of what School does as "wrong" and preached at it about what was "right." Such procedures are not effective in guiding children and will not be effective either in guiding educational innovation. School will not come to use computers "properly" because researchers tell it how to do so.

It will come to use them well (if it ever does) as an integral part of a coherent developmental process. Like good developmental teachers, researchers can contribute best if they understand change in School as development, and support this by transferring the ideas that were successful for understanding change in children.

Piaget vastly increased understanding of children by means of an idea that seems, as many of the greatest ideas do, ridiculously obvious once one has understood it. All mental operation, he said, has two facets, which he calls *assimilation* (changing your representation of the world to fit your ways of thinking) and *accommodation* (adapting your ways of thinking to fit the world). School's first response to the computer was, quite naturally, one of assimilation. School did not let itself change under the influence of the new device; it saw the computer through the mental lens of its own ways of thinking and doing. It is a characteristic of conservative systems that accommodation will come only when the opportunities of assimilation have been exhausted. In the interim one sees interesting subplots of the developmental story as the system displays its ability to block off incipient accommodations.

In education the acronym CAI (Computer Aided Instruction) is used for the fully assimilated usage of computer technology. CAI refers to programming the computer to administer the kinds of exercise traditionally given by a teacher at a blackboard, a textbook, or a worksheet. This is so far from challenging the assumptions of traditional School that critics frequently ask whether it does anything at all to justify the cost of computers. The most hardened skeptics describe the computer as "a thousand-dollar flash card," and what it does as "drill and kill."

Advocates reply by listing advantages of having a computer ask a student, for example, to calculate 35 percent of $2.00. Those most frequently cited include immediate feedback (one will learn more from a mistake by being told immediately not only that one is wrong but why); individualized instruction (the questions can be matched to the level of competence of the student); and neutrality (the computer is not subject to biased perceptions, by student of teacher and vice versa, related to race, gender, or personal history). Statistical studies show that the introduction of CAI will often modestly raise test scores, especially at the low end of the scale. But it does this without questioning the structure or the educational goals of traditional School.

The first sign of incipient accommodation came, as perhaps it always does, through another assimilation. Large numbers of progressive teachers were able to assimilate the computer to their ideas about teaching (and about getting around School), and this gave rise to a movement that I shall call the Progressive Educational Technology (or PET) Movement.

CAI is older than PET—in fact, it dates back almost as far as the idea of the computer. When I first entered the computer scene it was already in existence and, in fact, held a monopoly on thinking about computers in education. The first formulations of ideas that would become those of PET emerged slowly from the development of Logo and the turtle, mentioned in the last chapter. In the early 1970s this stream of development was joined by another under the leadership of Alan Kay, a computer scientist, musician, and inspiring personality who was, I believe, the first person to use the words *personal computer.* At the end of the 1970s, these ideas filtered slowly into the awareness of progressive teachers who happened also to be in touch with the excitement that accompanied the first microcomputers.

In 1980 three events came together to give a powerful boost to the awareness among teachers that computers could be used in the spirit of progressive education. *Mindstorms* set this out in easily accessible form, inexpensive personal computers reached a level of performance that could support a usable version of Logo, and Logo software became commercially available. The result was a grass-roots movement that generated many thousands of classroom implementations of PET. The character of this movement and the depth of its conflict with School's philosophy cannot be captured by abstract formulas. Instead, some anecdotes will convey the texture of the conflict.

Even now I can close my eyes and see a 1981 scene in a fifth-grade classroom in a New York City public school. Two worlds seemed to coexist in one room: At one end, a teacher, Thelma, was giving a "lesson" at the blackboard; at the other, a cluster of students was working with two computers. The computer group ran into a problem and sent someone to "ask the teacher." Thelma said, "Maybe Bill can help"—and continued her lesson without missing a beat, quite unperturbed by the fact that Bill had now joined the ranks of students who weren't even pretending to listen to her.

The front and the back of the room were separated by much more than a difference between the technology of the computer and the technology of the blackboard. A far greater difference marked the children's relationship with what they were doing. In front, they were following someone else's agenda; in the back, they were following their own. Among them, the ones I remember most vividly were Brian and Henry.

When I came into the room I was captured, as was every visitor, by the spectacular visual effects on the computer screen produced by programs written by the two students. Colored shapes moving in complex intertwining paths spoke immediately to a choreographic talent, a sense of movement and drama. I had to examine the display more closely before I was able to recognize the mathematical sophistication that went into controlling the geometry and dynamics of the movements. These boys were engaged in a mathematical exercise fundamentally different from calculating 35 percent of $2.00 on command. Their activity included such calculations (together with more sophisticated mathematical thinking) but not as set exercises; the calculations came up in the course of doing a larger and personally motivated project. In fact, I chose the percentage problem as my example to illustrate CAI expressly because it is quite like one of the many different kinds of calculational problem Brian and Henry did have to solve: For example, at what speeds do two objects have to move so as to arrive at the same place at the same time if one follows a path whose length is 35 percent of the length of the other?

This latter problem is harder than the usual School kind

because its geometric form makes it more complex and because the boys would have to scrounge and scurry to find out how to do it: ask a teacher or fellow student, look in a book, work by analogy with another situation, try to invent a method, resort to trial and error. Children never seem to mind: What makes School math repugnant for the Brians and boring for the Henrys is not that it is "hard" but that it is a senseless ritual dictated by the agenda of a set curriculum that says, "Today, because it is the fifteenth Monday of your fifth-grade year, you have to do this sum irrespective of who you are or what you really want to do; do what you are told and do it the way you are told to do it." The point is not that their teacher was willing, as some advocates of "free school" have proposed, to let her charges do anything they wanted. Far from it: She imposed very high standards and demanded commitment and discipline. But when Brian and Henry wanted to do something that was deeper, more instructive, and more intellectually demanding than the fifth-grade curriculum, her instinct as a teacher told her to encourage them.

The previous relationship between these boys says a great deal about School as an intellectual environment. Although these two boys had been classmates for four years, they hadn't talked to one another much until the computers brought them together. They had already developed strong individual interests in life, and although School threw them into the same room, it provided few opportunities for these interests to meld into real relationship. Thus School squanders its most valuable resource—the interchange between the most intellectually interesting students.

Henry had always been the math whiz and his fantasies were in science fiction; Brian had always cared about music and dance. Watching him, one had no doubt that the sensory and bodily aspects of the world were important to him. Henry was awkward in his movements, one might say out of touch with his body. He cared little about clothes and colors. But although this cut him off from a significant area of experience, up to the arrival of the computers he had not experienced it as a defi- ciency—certainly not as a deficiency relevant to his schoolwork. Science and mathematics, the areas he enjoyed and excelled in most, seemed to have no relationship with sensory enjoyment and physical action. Indeed, this perception surely contributed to his attachment to these activities, just as it contributed to Henry's indifferent response to them.

When their teacher brought computers to the classroom, there- fore, the two students had very different expectations. Henry knew instantly that this was going to be his thing; without any doubt he would be "best at computer." Brian's reaction mixed a mild curiosity with a twinge of apprehension.

Henry found that the route to making the most of the com- puter went through establishing a working relationship with the least likely person in the class, Brian the dancer. Brian found for the first time that mathematics could be a personally exciting medium of self-expression and the basis of a genuinely interest- ing friendship.

The story needs some background information about how the computers were introduced into the classroom. Thelma had at- tended a summer workshop sponsored by the National Science Foundation on using computers in schools. She had enrolled with little idea of what she would do there, and with some trepidation, for she had never thought of herself as a "technology person." But computers were in the air. She had friends who spoke about the microcomputer revolution, about how these new machines would give ordinary citizens access to information previously monopolized by big corporations and government agencies. She had read that they would lead to new methods of teaching. But, most important, she understood that children loved them, and the same spirit that led her to bring hamsters and plants and posters and all manner of what she called "junk" into her classroom sparked her interest when she heard about the summer course.

Thelma's first contact with computer programming consisted of using Logo to instruct the computer to draw patterns of lines on its screen. She was actually surprised at her surprise at finding that she could make the computer draw something she wanted; even getting it to draw a simple square gave her a sense of pleasure at beginning to "own" a technology so symbolic of what was most modern and most powerful. After a few days her ability to produce more intricate patterns and set objects in motion on the screen evoked associations with computer art and with the special effects in movies like *Star Wars*.

By bringing this kind of programming technique back to her classroom, Thelma inspired the collaboration between Brian and Henry. In her class, creating animation on the screen became the most common choice made by children who were free to do what they wished with the computers.

Some children created realistic animations to tell a story. Not surprisingly, Henry was among those who preferred more stylized forms whose visual interest was in the complexity of shapes and patterns of motion rather than a narrative content. Henry quickly understood the technical side of programming. Earlier than anyone else in the class, he knew exactly how to create figures on the screen and make them move. He had enough visual imagination to try for effects whose nature is evoked by the names he gave them: "Fireworks" or "Star Wars" or "The Big Bang." His talent for mathematics paid off in his easy mastery of techniques for programming an object on the screen to begin moving almost imperceptibly and then gradually accelerate. Something more creative showed itself in what a mathematician would call "generalizing the idea," when he realized that the same techniques could be used to make a sound mount in pitch from a low growl to a high scream and eventually disappear into the ultrasonic range. From a School point of view he was doing very well indeed, but something was missing.

Henry took pleasure in the mathematical cleverness behind his displays but was disappointed by the total effect. His problem was not simply that fellow students drew more "oohs" and "aahs" when they showed their work. He could feel that his creations lacked something he did not know how to achieve or even name, certain qualities that another fifth-grade student described as "grace" and "excitement." Perhaps for the first time in his life, he felt the pang of awareness of an intellectual limitation. His mind was ready for a breakthrough.

The idea came to him when he saw Brian dancing in a school corridor. Recognizing that Brian's movements had just what his screen displays lacked, Henry was led quickly to the inspired thought that they might work together to produce the best screen choreography ever made! The thought led to a long-term working relationship. Together the two boys created something that neither could even imagine alone, and in doing so learned much more than math test scores are capable of measuring.

They certainly mastered a great deal of technical mathematics. Moving those objects on the screen required a description of the movements in mathematical language that went beyond even Henry's previous knowledge. They represented an object's speed as a variable, and then set up formulas to vary it. They learned to think of directions as angles measured in degrees. They picked up the idea of doing geometry by coordinates in a way much closer to the living and personal discovery through which René Descartes first came upon it than to the deadly formal presentation of math textbooks. But this kind of knowledge was only a small part of what they learned.

Beyond developing technical mathematical skills, they came to experience mathematics in a very different way. It became something to be used purposefully; they felt it as a source of power in pursuing important and deeply personal projects. I am not sure that people who have not experienced mathematics in this way can fully appreciate how heady, how powerful, it can be. An analogy might be the experience of learning to ski. At first one is instructed in a series of awkward movements: Shift your weight, bend your knees, and so on. One obeys the commands but it feels as if one is clumsily acting at being someone else. Then one day comes a conversion experience. One is flying (or so it seems) down the slope. One's own knees are flexing and extending, one's own weight is shifting. One doesn't have to "do" these things; they flow as inseparable parts of a fluent and joyous movement.

Certainly for Brian and possibly for Henry too, their collaborative work had elements of such a conversion experience. Mathematics became more like flying down the hill than like bending one's knees and shifting one's weight at the command of an instructor. This does not mean that doing mathematics became easy: Quite the contrary, just as in the experience of skiing, there was the frustration and never-ending struggle of mastering new techniques and handling new challenges. It became harder as they engaged with more serious problems, but when one is deeply involved in something, "easy" is not what one wants. If it were, one would spend the rest of one's skiing life going down the easiest slopes; but most people, especially young people, seek the challenge of moving on to more interesting terrain.

The analogy with skiing brings out an experiential side of Brian's and Henry's mathematical learning that goes beyond acquiring technical knowledge. The analogy also suggests ways in which their learning went beyond mathematical learning even in the widest sense of mathematics. The use of the word *fluent* in reference to skiing reflects a relationship with activities where the word is more often applied, for example, language or musical performance. I want to generalize this notion to other activities and suggest that Henry and Brian, in rather different ways, were learning to be fluent in the use of mathematics. They were also learning the feel of fluency. I want to suggest that fluency in its own right is an important and insufficiently recognized area of competence.

Brian came to the collaboration with certain kinds of fluency. His fluency in dance, in body movement, was what drew Henry's attention and what provided the basis of the collaboration. But there was more to the pattern of where he was and was not fluent than simple competence in dance. Brian was a fluent talker; he could tell a story in a way that would hold rapt attention. His talking had exactly those qualities of "grace" and "excitement" that were missing in Henry's programming. But an amazing thing happened when he took a pencil to write. What came out was totally lacking in these qualities. What he put on paper was one laboriously wooden sentence after another. The contrast of oral fluency with plodding writing is extremely common and a major cause of illiteracy: Those who know from their oral skills what it is like to use language fluently are repelled by their own clumsiness when forced to write and often end up simply refusing to do it.

For people like Brian, the opportunity to make animations provides a way to extend their domain of fluency into an area that shares essential qualities with speech, body movement, and written language. It may take time to get your screen creation right, but once you do you can move with it; you can feel its excitement in a very direct bodily way. On the other hand, the program is a text that stays still to be examined and edited. In this way it is like writing; indeed, it is writing.

This is the first of many ways in which the computer breaks down the barriers that traditionally separate the preletterate from the letterate, the concrete from the abstract, the bodily from the disembodied. By straddling these divisions it removes an obstacle that has kept many people from crossing from the concrete, body-syntonic orality of childhood to forms of competence that have in the past been accessible only in literate, abstract, and decorporalized forms. This applies most directly to Brian. Henry's most obvious problems with this crossing are seen in the opposite sense: He had moved easily but too thoroughly to the other side and cannot easily come back.

Our culture's supervaluation of the abstract obscures the ways in which Henry may have benefited from his exposure to thinking about the choreography of movements. Acquiring a feel for creating grace and excitement would have stood him in good stead for writing a science report, composing a story, or simply telling a joke. Given time, it could even have affected the way he moved his body. It might have changed his social life. More subtly and more profoundly, it might have opened him to a greater variety of ways of knowing.

Both boys felt what it was like to communicate with one another across a cultural barrier. They had the experience of jointly managing a complex project over many weeks, and, of course—though this in itself was the least of it—they were learning to program computers.

The story of Brian and Henry is not intended to suggest that all students who encounter Logo will have a similar experience. Many other factors besides "Logo" entered into what happened. Perhaps one could sum them up by saying that the teacher succeeded in creating a productive and supportive computer culture in her classroom. And even then, conditions were far from ideal. Many children will have an experience that is less rich, though it is rare that nothing is gained. The story is not meant to be statistically representative of an average event but conceptually representative of a mode of learning very different from School's. The next story is similarly representative of School's "immune response."

Richard had an intensive Logo experience in his fourth- and fifth-grade years at the Hennigan Elementary School in Boston. In the experimental Project Headlight, he had used Logo almost every school day in the spirit shown by Brian and Henry, and had acquired a considerable competence both in the technical aspects of Logo programming and in the spirit of using it as a medium for other work. A few months after Richard graduated from Hennigan, he was visited at his new school by members of the research team who had worked with him and were interested in his progress. Although the researchers knew that access to computers at the new school was much more limited than at Hennigan, they also knew that a large part of this time was devoted to Logo and were looking forward to seeing what Richard was doing with his proficiency in Logo. To their surprise, they were told that he was not allowed to do it. "But we thought you liked Logo," they said to the teacher. "Yes I do," she replied, "and I have my students spend a lot of time on it. But Richard already knows Logo. So I had him learn something else."

The story captures one of the chief differences between learning at school and all other learning. Generally in life, knowledge is acquired to be used. But school learning more often fits Freire's apt metaphor: Knowledge is treated like money, to be put away in a bank for the future. Something of this way of thinking was present in the attitude of the computer teacher at Richard's new school. Logo is something to be learned rather than something to be used; the students learn it in order to know it; when they know it they put it away in their memory banks (which, incidentally, pay no interest) and go on to the next topic in the curriculum. In the case of computer knowledge, the banking approach is often defended by the argument that it will stand the students in good stead when they grow up and look for jobs that will require computer skills. Nothing could be more ridiculous. If "computer skill" is interpreted in a narrow sense of technical knowledge about computers, there is nothing the children can learn now that is worth banking: By the time they grow up, the computer skills required in the workplace will have evolved into something fundamentally different. But what makes the argument truly ridiculous is that the very idea of banking computer knowledge for use one day in the workplace undermines the only really important "computer skill": the skill and habit of using the computer in doing whatever one is doing. But this is exactly what was given up in shifting the computer into the computer lab.

Another way in which computers can be either integrated into or isolated from the learning process has to do less with the computer as an instrument than with computing as a set of ideas. The issue appears very clearly when one contrasts what has come to be called "computer literacy" with the sense of the word *literacy* used to refer to someone as a literate person. *Computer literacy* has come to be defined, especially in the context of School, as a very minimal practical knowledge about computers. Someone who had so minimal a level of knowledge of reading, writing, and literature would be called illiterate; the same considerations ought to lead us to call someone who has an equally minimal knowledge about computers computer-illiterate. Moreover, the difference is not merely one of degree but of one of kinds of knowledge. When we say "X is a very literate person," we do not mean that X is highly skilled at deciphering phonics. At the least, we imply that X knows literature, but beyond this we mean that X has certain ways of understanding the world that derive from an acquaintance with literary culture. In the same way, the term *computer literacy* should refer to the kinds of knowing that derive from a computer culture.

An illustration of this point is provided by a teaching unit designed by teacher Joanne Ronkin at the Hennigan School that combines studying the structure of flowers with studying the structure of computer programs. The two go together intimately and in very simple ways. The student has to make a computer program to draw a flower; the structured style of programming would suggest dividing the job into writing "subprocedures" for the different parts of the flower. The student is then faced with the choice of doing this in a way that matches the structure of the flower or in a way that does not. In my own programming style I tend to be relatively unstructured unless there is a strong reason: One such reason would impel me to be very structured about a flower program, because I see the "design" of the flower as fitting the structured precepts. In fact, I think that the reason for the two structures is much the same. A strong argument for modularized programs is that they facilitate debugging, and it seems plausible to me that the modular structure of biological systems facilitates "debugging" in the course of evolution. This is a small example, but a pregnant one, of how seeing the world through computational concepts leads to insights into familiar phenomena that have no direct connection with computers.

The criticism of the computer lab as neutralizing the computer is not to be taken as denying that computers in a room apart can be used in wonderful ways—so long as the room apart is allowed to become the meeting point of ideas that were previously kept separate.

In a junior high school in Missouri, an unlikely set of teachers got together to develop a joint educational project: the physics teacher, the physical education teacher, and the shop teacher. They intended to develop a workshop for students on robotics, a topic with aspects that appealed to each of the three teachers. The physics teacher was interested in some underlying theoretical issues, the physical education teacher in body movements, and the shop teacher in machine construction.

The project had an importance beyond what was specifically learned in the robotics workshop. The fact that these three teachers were doing something together carried a message for students, a message that one could formulate much too crudely as recognizing that "nerds" and "jocks" might have more in common than they think.

The robotics project provides a simple example of what I call second-order effects or systemic effects of the computer presence. The school did not spend thousands of dollars on computers specifically so that students could have the experience of witnessing a spontaneous alliance among three teachers from strongly separate departments. Computers are usually introduced to achieve specific educational objectives, and their first-order effects are measured by looking at how well these objectives are achieved. But, to an extent that varies enormously from school to school, the computer presence can come to play a less specific, but potentially more powerful, role: By entering the culture of the school it can weave itself into learning in many more ways than its original promoters could possibly have anticipated.

The African textiles project mentioned in chapter 1 illustrates another important way in which a computer lab can give rise to better results than the administration planned or paid for. The teacher, Orlando Mihich, is one of many I have known who contributed personal time to organize sessions in the computer lab outside of school hours, allowing at least some students to work with the computers freely enough for a genuine learning experience. Some of the best examples of computer-based learning projects came from the individual initiative of creative teachers who refused the narrow role of "computer teacher."

Despite many examples of such excellent work, the isolation of the computer presence must be seen as a kind of immune response of School to a foreign body; whether or not the participants were aware that this is what they were doing, it is clear that the logic of the process was to bring the intrusive thing back into line with School's ways. The computer in the classroom was undermining the division of knowledge into subjects; it was turned into a subject of its own. It undermined the idea of curriculum; it was made the topic of a curriculum of its own. But, of course, this mechanism is not confined to computers. In its time, School has normalized other subversive influences too. For example, Piaget was the theorist of learning without curriculum; School spawned the project of developing a Piagetian curriculum.

By recognizing such immune reactions, we are led to seek answers to the question, "Why is there no megachange?" by specifically searching out mechanisms that defend School against megachange. To the extent that we find such mechanisms, we can then start thinking about School in ways that will enable us to foster change more effectively. Thus, the story of Brian and Henry once more enables us to see the tension between the teacher's way and School's way of handling the computer. Developing insight into this tension is a central theme of this book. What is School's way? What is the teacher's way?

I go back to the comparison between education and fields such as medicine, which have undergone megachange. One possible response to the question of why there has not been megachange in education is to argue that the very idea of megachange is inappropriate to education: School is essentially different from examples of megachanged fields like surgery. Surgery, according to this argument, is susceptible to technologically induced mega-change because it is an essentially technical act. But learning is a natural act, like eating, for example, or face-to-face conversation. There have been changes in eating habits, but not megachange. Time travelers from a distant past would certainly have no problem recognizing that we are eating even if they fail to recognize the ingredients. The act of eating is essentially the same whether the food is cooked in microwave ovens, over open fires, or not at all. If there are megadifferences in eating, they lie in the social and not in the technical dimensions.

I would agree that learning is a natural act if we are talking about the kind of learning that happens in a healthy relationship between a mother and her baby or between two people getting to know each other. But schooling is not a natural act. Quite the contrary: The institution of School, with its daily lesson plans, fixed curriculum, standardized tests, and other such paraphernalia tends constantly to reduce learning to a series of technical acts and the teacher to the role of a technician. Of course, it never fully succeeds, for teachers resist the role of technician and bring warm, natural human relationships into their classrooms. But what is important for thinking about the potential for megachange is that this situation places the teacher in a state of tension between two poles: School tries to make the teacher into a technician; in most cases a sense of self resists, though in many the teacher will have internalized School's concept of teaching. Each teacher is therefore somewhere along the continuum between technician and what I dare call a true teacher.

The central issue of change in education is the tension between technicalizing and not technicalizing, and here the teacher occupies the fulcrum position.

Not since the printing press has there been so great a surge in the potential to boost technicalized learning. But there is also another side: Paradoxically, the same technology has the potential to detechnicalize learning. Were this to happen, I would count it as a far larger change than the appearance on every desk of a computer programmed to lead the student through the paces of the same old curriculum. But it is not necessary to quibble about which change is more far-reaching. What is necessary is to recognize that the great issue in the future of education is whether technology will strengthen or undermine the technicalness of what has became the theoretical model, and to a large extent the reality, of School. My paradoxical argument is that technology can support megachange in education as far-reaching as what we have seen in medicine, but it will do this through a process directly opposite to what has driven change in modern medicine. Medicine has changed by becoming more and more technical in its nature; in education, change will come by using technical means to shuck off the technical nature of School learning.

4

• • •

Teachers

THERE was a time when I believed, as many people do, that teachers would be the most difficult obstacle in the way of transforming School.* This simplistic belief, whose insistent presence is in reality a far greater obstacle to educational change than the fact that some teachers actually are conservative, can be traced back to deeply rooted cultural representations. In my case, I remember being impressed in junior high by George Bernard Shaw's cynical aphorism: "He who can, does; he who cannot, teaches." Someone who "cannot" is not likely to be a constructive partner in bringing about major change.

Culturally shared negative attitudes toward teachers are nourished by personal experiences. As a rebellious child I saw teachers as the enemy. Then, with time, these feelings merged with a theoretical position which had the illogical consequence of further demonizing teachers by identifying them with the roles that School forced on them. I disliked School's coercive methods, and it was the teachers who applied the coercion. I disapproved of judgment by grading, and it was the teacher who gave the grades.

*The ideas in this chapter took shape in conversations with Carol Sperry.

Yet I certainly had grounds in early experience for a more sympathetic view of teachers.

Like most people with generally bad memories of school, I have some wonderful impressions of individual teachers. For example, Mr. Wallis has lost none of his presence. "Daisy" (as we called him, though not to his face) officially taught me Latin and Greek, but gave me far more insight into Lewis Caroll than Cicero or Herodotus. He also left me with an eleventh commandment: "Thou shalt invent three theories every day before breakfast and throw them away before dinner." I loved him, and see even now that I am indebted to him for at least some strands of the playful epistemological stance that informs my present thinking. But at the time, and until recently, I classed Daisy as an exception, thus leaving my antiteacher prejudice as entire as the racism of those who say: "Me? Why, some of my best friends are. . . ." The net effect was not to think better of teachers but to say, "Daisy's no teacher, he's a real mensch." I had to write *Mindstorms* and develop Logo to find out how many other teachers are, too; it is School that disguises them as something else.

Logo gave many thousands of elementary teachers their first opportunity to appropriate the computer in ways that would extend their personal styles of teaching. This was not easy for them. They were frustrated by poor conditions: They usually had to work with minimal computer systems and often had to share them among several classrooms; opportunities to develop their own computer knowledge were limited; and School's immune response often snatched away the successes they did achieve. Even the Logo they had in those days looks sadly primitive when I look back on it from the perspective of another decade of growth of the language. More recent versions of Logo are far more user-friendly, intuitive, and flexible. But although only a minority of these pioneering teachers succeeded in using Logo to build a satisfying classroom environment, what they tried to do is a rich source for understanding the force for change latent in their profession. It turned my own thinking around completely. One thinks of a book as a vehicle through which the readers come to understand how the author thinks. *Mindstorms* worked for me in the opposite direction as well.

I had not written the book with teachers in mind; at most, I imagined it being read by a small vanguard among them. So when the estimated number of teacher readers climbed into six digits, I was pleased but perturbed. What did they like in my book? It was troubling that there was something about my own work I did not understand.

Fortunately, the book also helped me find answers to the questions it raised. It was a passport into the world of teachers. I received hundreds of letters from teachers telling me about their yearnings and hopes, their plans and resentments. I was flooded with invitations to give speeches and seminars, visit schools, and participate in projects. All this offered a special opportunity to understand what teachers were expressing in their experiments with computers. As I did so, my identification of "teacher" with "School" slowly dissolved into a perception of a far more complex relationship. The shift brought both a liberating sense that the balance of forces was more favorable to change than I had supposed and, at the same time, a new challenge to understand the interplay of currents in the world of teachers that favor change and that resist it. Finding ways to support the evolution of these currents may be among the most important contributions one can make to promote educational change.

As background to understanding these currents, I begin by looking at a story recounted by education writer Fred Hechinger in a sorely missed *New York Times* column. I cannot imagine a teacher who will not hear in the story the echo of some personal experience.

The principal of a New York school dropped in to listen to a chemistry class. The lesson was brilliant. The principal was enthralled. After the class he congratulated the teacher on a superb piece of teaching, and then asked to see his lesson plan. The teacher replied that since he knew this material so well and cared about it so much, he didn't think he needed a lesson plan. The principal clearly had no complaint about the lesson itself, but the teacher was guilty of not following procedures and had a letter of reprimand placed in his file.

There is more than one way to read this poignant account of a system defeating its own purposes in the attempt to enforce them. One can take it as a satirico-comic account of a run-in between an overzealous supervisor and a naïve worker, the former ridiculously literal-minded about a minor transgression of the letter of the rules and the latter refusing to understand the importance of appearances, which could have been saved by writing a token lesson plan. On this reading, the story is only incidentally about School; it could be matched by bureaucracy stories from other walks of life.

On another reading, however, the story touches the nerve of what School is really about. It evokes tensions between a warm idea of School as a nurturing place for children and a chilling idea of School as a machine to perform laid-down procedures. It evokes yearnings for teaching that will help us fall in love with knowledge, and frustrations at being made to learn lists of facts, loved or not, that experts have decided must be known.

The choice between these readings of Hechinger's story reflects the central question about education: Is the trouble with school a superficial one that could be fixed by a good dose of good will and common sense, or is it a deep flaw in the foundational assumptions on which the entire system is built? Is School's malady a cold or a cancer?

The meaning of these two views is brought out by comparing Hechinger's incident with my central example from the previous chapter. School has evolved a hierarchical system of control that sets narrow limits within which the actors—administrators as well as teachers—are allowed to exercise a degree of personal initiative. Neither side ever fully accepts these limits. The Hechinger story shows a border skirmish in a permanent struggle for power in which participants constantly test their strength without actually challenging the system itself. The seeds of a sharper challenge were present in the decision to allow Brian and Henry to spend their time on computer choreography. The chemistry teacher could, had he wished, have written a token lesson plan, as many of his colleagues routinely do. Thelma did not have this option. There could not be a lesson plan for the simple reason that there was no "lesson."

Thus the original decision about how to use computers placed the teacher on a collision course with School's system of control: As soon as she decided not to control the students, she took away School's established way of controlling her. The question has moved from how power is distributed within the educational hierarchy to whether hierarchy is an appropriate mode of organization for education. There are activities where hierarchical organization is obligatory: The military is an obvious example. At another extreme there are activities where any sensible person would judge hierarchical organization to be absurd, for example, in poetry or painting. In other areas there is room for choice in the balance between hierarchy and its opposite—for which I follow Warren McCulloch in using the name *heterarchy,* which suggests a system in which each element is equally ruled by all others. Where on this spectrum between soldiering and poetry should one place the organization of a school?

There is a danger of thinking about this as a "management problem" that a school could address (and many do) by bringing in a general-purpose expert on how to run organizations. But injecting a new management plan into an otherwise unchanged School is like injecting computers or a new curriculum while leaving everything else unaltered. The foreign body will be rejected. School's hierarchical organization is intimately tied to its view of education and in particular to its commitment to hierarchical ways of thinking about knowledge itself. What one will consider to be the proper place for School on the heterarchy-hierarchy scale of organizational forms depends on the location of one's theory of knowledge on the heterarchy-hierarchy scale of epistemologies.

A caricatured hierarchical theory of knowledge and of school might run something as follows: Knowledge is made of atomic pieces called facts and concepts and skills. A good citizen needs to possess 40,000 of these atoms. Children can acquire 20 atoms per day. A little calculation shows that 180 days a year for 12 years will be sufficient to get 43,200 atoms into their heads—but the operation will have to be well organized, for while some overrun on time can be absorbed, as little as 10 percent would make it impossible to achieve the goal. It follows that the technicians in charge (hereafter called teachers) have to follow a careful plan (hereafter called the curriculum) that is coordinated over the entire 12 years. They must therefore be required to write down each day which atoms they have delivered into the students' memory banks. The problem of quality control is facilitated by the discovery that there are hierarchical relations among the atoms: Facts fall under concepts, concepts can be classified as subjects, and subjects split up as grade levels. A hierarchy of people can be constructed to match the hierarchy of knowledge. Teachers can be supervised by curriculum coordinators and department heads, these by principals, and these in turn by superintendents.

Such a theory might appeal to the analogy of building a Gothic cathedral out of 40,000 blocks of stone. Clearly, strict organization is needed to perform such a task. One cannot have individual workers deciding that they want to put a block here or there just because they are inspired to do so. Educating a child is a similar process. Everyone has to follow the plan.

Of course, nobody would subscribe to these theories in a literal sense. Yet I honestly believe that they capture the essence of the academically respectable theories from which the hierarchical organization of School derives its legitimacy. If the Gothic cathedral model of learning were true in principle, Thelma would have been courting disaster by letting the children in her class decide, so to speak, where to place bricks; and the administration of her school would have been severely remiss for allowing her to do so. But she was not being lax, lazy, or irresponsible. Teachers who give so much autonomy to their students are thereby declaring their belief in a radically different theory of knowledge, one that entails far more work for them as well as for their students.

My use of the term "theory of knowledge" rather than "method of teaching" is deliberate. Progressive educators do not see themselves as offering an alternative way for students to learn the same list of items of knowledge. They value a different kind of knowledge.

For example, I occasionally use an elevator that has a security code. One has to key in a four-digit number before it will move. Since the code is changed frequently and I use the elevator only rarely, I usually remember each new code in a vague form. "There's a 17 and a 34," I say to myself; "perhaps it is 1734 or 3417, or maybe the numbers are 71 and 43." I make a few tries and the elevator moves. I think that's fine. It works. In school, however, I would fail the elevator-skills test. This is a trivial example of an important phenomenon that I call knowledge-in-use. When knowledge is doled out in tiny pieces, one can't do anything except memorize it in class and write it down in the test. When it is embedded in a context of use, one can push it around and fix minor bugs such as reversing the digits of the elevator code.

I am not suggesting that knowledge-in-use is the essence of progressive epistemology or even that every progressive teacher would accept this principle. I am using it here only as an example of a "different kind of knowledge." What teachers who reject School's philosophy of education actually believe varies widely. In fact, every teacher should be encouraged to go as far as possible toward developing a personal style of teaching. A less specific metaphor that I used in *Mindstorms,* however, does seem to capture a widely shared element well enough to provide a framework for looking more closely at the aspirations and problems of progressive teachers. The basis of the metaphor was an observation about the idea that children display "aptitudes" for their various school subjects. It is thoroughly embedded in our culture that some of us have a head for figures while most don't, and accordingly, most people think of themselves as not mathematically minded. But what do we say about children who have trouble learning French in American schools?

Whatever the explanation of their difficulty, one certainly cannot ascribe it to a lack of aptitude for French—we can be sure that most of these children would have learned French perfectly well had they been born and raised in France. Perhaps they lack an aptitude for learning French as it is taught in American schools, but that is a different matter altogether. In the same way, we have no better reason to suppose that these children who have trouble with math lack mathematical intelligence than to suppose that the others lack "French intelligence." We are left with the question: What would happen if children who can't do math grew up in Mathland, a place that is to math what France is to French? Many teachers accepted the challenge to build something like a Mathland in their classrooms, and took Logo and its turtle as building material. Thelma's classroom shows in a general way how many went about doing this. Following this metaphor, one can think of Brian and Henry as being in Mathland; what they were doing with the computer was more like learning French in France, while what happened in the regular math class was more like learning math as a foreign language. In these computer contexts, as in learning French in France, the learner can begin by knowing something in a very fumbly sort of way before it becomes established. In the math class, where knowledge is not used but simply piled up like the bricks forming a dead building, there is no room for significant experimenting.

Many progressive teachers might have doubts about whether creating a Mathland is really feasible and hesitations about what inconveniences it might bring if it is; but leaving aside practical considerations, it seems obvious to them that learning French in France and math in Mathland is in principle a better way than those of the traditional classroom.

The immediate consequence for the practice of teaching is the one I have already noted. The learning of a dead subject requires a technical act of carving the knowledge into teachable bites so that they can be fed to the students one at a time by a teacher, and this leads straight into the traditional paraphernalia of curriculum, hierarchy, and control. By contrast, Brian and Henry were able to find their own way to structure their knowledge with only occasional advice. Learning-in-use liberates the students to learn in a personal way, and this in turn liberates teachers to offer their students something more personal and more rewarding for both sides. But this prospect does not come without problems, and some teachers will see it more as a threat than as a liberation.

Thelma's rewarding feeling that she had exercised a creative (and unintentionally subversive) act in setting up her plan for computers brought psychological as well as bureaucratic risk. School's definition of roles and procedures restricts the teacher but also offers protection, as we see in the following story whose main features I have heard from many who have taken the same course as Thelma.

The following is a reconstruction of what I heard from Joe, a fifth-grade teacher:

From the time the computers came I began to be afraid of the day my students would know more about programming than I ever will. Of course, at the beginning I had a big advantage. I came fresh from a summer workshop on Logo, and the students were just beginning. But during the year they were catching up. They were spending more time on it than I could. Actually, they didn't catch up the first year. But I knew that each year the children would know more because they would have had experience in previous grades. Besides, children are more in tune with computers than we grown-ups.

The first few times I noticed that the students had problems I couldn't even understand, let alone solve, I struggled to avoid facing the fact that I could not keep up my stance of knowing more than they did. I was afraid that giving it up would undermine my authority as a teacher. But the situation became worse. Eventually I broke down and said I didn't understand the problem—go discuss it with some of the others in the class who might be able to help. Which they did. And it turned out that together the kids could figure out a solution. Now the amazing thing is that what I was afraid of turned out to be a liberation. I no longer had to fear being exposed. I was. I no longer had to pretend. And the wonderful thing was that I realized that my bluff was called for more than computers. I felt I could no longer pretend to know everything in other subjects as well. What a relief! It has changed my relationship with the children and with myself. My class has become much more of a collaborative community where we are all learning together.

Reflection on this story will show that there is no simple answer to some obvious quantitative questions that some readers must by now have asked: How many teachers fit the optimistic description of Thelma? How far would they take these ideas? How much effort and sacrifice would they make? My description gives Thelma the purity of a rare dedicated idealist. Many more have the doubts, the fears, and the ambivalence that Joe shares with most of the teachers who were drawn to experiment with computers as an instrument of change. Joe embarked on the experiment with trepidation. He did not fully see in advance what problems he would have, and when they came up he hesitated. Events turned out well in his case, but most others in his position balked and retreated. Many had their computers merged into computer labs. Some followed them, giving up the classroom to become computer teachers. Many felt seduced and abandoned by the talk of a computer revolution as the use of the computer became routinized. Just how many stayed in and how many dropped out is too hard to determine and would, in any case, not be worth knowing since we see from Joe's account that the individual case depends on a fragile balance that can tip one way or the other. What is certainly of no value whatsoever for those interested in change is to play down the adverse factors: Only by understanding them can we craft sensible strategies for the future. By the same token, they give little grounds for comfort to those who still predict that computers do not have a significant future in education.

Despite his doubts, Joe went further than the others I have mentioned so far. Hechinger's chemistry teacher tried to express his own intellectual enthusiasm in his teaching; Thelma tried to create an environment in which children would develop their own enthusiasms; Joe took a further step by explicitly formulating the idea (which the others may have had tacitly) of joining the fun as a co-learner with his students. The progression is psychologically understandable. Wanting to learn is a basic human desire, and being with children who are doing it while being deprived oneself is like being a dieter watching the diners in a fine restaurant. Why don't all teachers do it?

Many aspects of School block teachers from the fulfillment of functioning in a class as co-learners. The mundane matter of schedule is most often mentioned if one asks progressive teachers. They say that there simply is not enough time. I think Joe shows the fallacy in this explanation, however. There would indeed not be enough time for him to keep everything else and also get in his own learning. But he had the courage to implement a plan with a better chance of working: He changed the life of his class in such a way that students could give as well as take, and his learning was not competitive with theirs but contributed to it. To do this he had to face something that it took courage to admit: Most of the work he made his students do was too boring to entice him to join in! The computer changed the situation because it itself is an interesting object to learn about and because it added dimensions of interest to other areas of work.

What I actually saw Joe doing with his class involved a much broader range of learning than the technical aspects of computer programming that had been the object of his fears. Some of his students were doing work like Brian and Henry, but most were engaged in projects of a very different kind in which mathematics was integrated into fact-oriented subjects such as history or science. An aspect of these projects was something I first saw in the work of a fourth- and fifth-grade teacher at the Hennigan School in Boston.

Before computers entered her life, Joanne had developed a project as part of her classwork on human biology. The topic of study was the skeleton, and her style of handling it was to ask the students to choose a bone and make a report on it. When the computers came she simply did what she had always done, except that the students knew enough Logo by then to make their report on the computer screen instead of using pencil and paper. In one sense nothing changed except for a shift of media. But the shift had consequences. One of these was related to the fears ex-

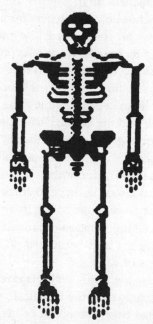

This picture was generated by a LogoWriter program written by four fourth-grade students.

pressed by Joe. The computer is an open-ended technical device that incites at least some students to push their knowledge to the limit to enhance the project through an unlimited variety of "effects"; thus learning more about computer techniques becomes part of the project in a way that had not happened with pencil and paper. This might seem to distract from the "main purpose," which was studying biology. It did not: Thinking about representations on the screen produced a richer engagement with the skeleton than had been usual in the precomputer days. The skeleton illustrated, the collaborative work of four students, shows several features that are typical of what happens in a computer context.

First, the students transformed the assignment of representing a bone into one of representing the entire skeleton, a goal that was made possible by the fact that the computer allowed much better conditions of work: Parts made by the collaborators could be put together more easily. A close look will show that modules could be used in several places, and most important, changes would be made easily without the messy process of erasing or the tedious one of starting over. Second, these same working conditions facilitated a double intention that is clearly visible in this object: The figure was made with an eye to visual aesthetics as well as to scientific accuracy. This raises challenging issues about the nature of knowledge and the criteria for judging it. I would call it an epistemological responsibility of the teacher to enter into discussion with these students (which in fact I had the privilege of doing) about what was sacrificed in each for the sake of the other. There can be no absolute answer, but there can be articulate and thoughtful discussion.

The issue of science and aesthetics is just one of many that make a different kind of demand on—and offer a richer kind of opportunity to—a teacher than is usual in a science class. Whether this is seen as a demand or as an opportunity, it certainly requires knowledge and sophistication for which there is no place in the course catalog of the typical school of education.

Where can teachers find help in developing themselves in these directions? What kind of development would help them?

To define this problem, which may be the most important of all those facing the adoption of computers in education, it might help to review some of the obstacles faced by teachers who try to find a solution. The most brutal of these simply prevents the interesting situation from arising. The designers of the skeleton had access to computers for about one hour a day, and their regular teacher had the freedom to use this time as she wished. Thus they and the teacher could be immersed in the project sufficiently for interesting issues to come up and be dealt with in an interesting way.

The odds are against anything like this happening—though it is a tribute to the amazing resilience of students and teachers that it sometimes does—when students have forty minutes a week of computer lab and learn about word processing, data bases, and what's in the computer, as well as "do a little Logo." A second obstacle is the concept of teacher training. Although the name is not what is most important about this concept, it is curious that the phrase "teacher training" comes trippingly off the tongues of people who would be horrified at the suggestion that teachers are being trained to "train" children. The phrase makes me think of toilet training, basic training, and tiger training. I know that the word *training* is often used for respectable kinds of learning. For example, I said in the second chapter that I was trained as a mathematician. But justifying "teacher training" in this way feels to me—and to quite a number of teachers I know—like justifying the use of the pronoun *he* on the grounds that it embraces woman. On purely abstract linguistic grounds both usages are "correct," but in both cases what is involved is not an issue of syntax but one of ideology. Why the asymmetry? Why do we talk about teachers and children so differently? The answer brings me back to my main theme: School does not have in its institutional mind that teachers have a creative role; it sees them as technicians doing a technical job, and for this the word *training* is perfectly appropriate.

Whether or not one accepts this analysis in general, it is hard not to recognize its truth in the kind of preparation School generally considers appropriate for computer teachers. In many school systems, what the teachers who will use the computers are offered in preparation is quite appropriately called training, for it consists of a small number of two-hour sessions, misnamed "workshops" or "seminars," whose goal is to impart technical skills. To highlight the limitation, it is worth looking at two examples of providing better conditions for teachers to learn and grow.

About eight years ago I conducted a summer workshop on Logo for a small group of teachers. I was a little nervous because I suspected that one of the participants was there not out of commitment to learning Logo but because she was under orders from a principal who wanted a computer project in his school at a time when that was still something exceptional. I knew that a single participant's bottled-up resentment at losing summer vacation time could poison the spirit of the group, even if the others had come out of a personal desire to learn.

One of my preferred styles of working with such a group is to propose a form of project sufficiently open to allow very different approaches and sufficiently restricted to allow the different approaches to be compared. In this workshop I proposed that everyone write a program to represent some aspect of the notion of "village." Programming the computer to draw a village on the screen presents itself as a good theme for beginners to exercise techniques of programming. One can start by writing a procedure to draw a single dwelling; once this is debugged, it can be used as subprocedure for a superprocedure to obtain a group of identical dwellings; and having obtained a product, one can go on to introduce variability and add all manner of frills and details including animation, text, and hypertext. From a teaching point of view, it has the advantage that students can stop at different levels, matching their technical abilities and personal tastes, and yet all have something to show for the work.

As the days went on, my fears did not seem to be founded. Everyone was caught up in the activity. I was especially relieved to observe that the member of the group I had thought would be most difficult seemed hardly able to contain her excitement. In every discussion period she bubbled over with ideas about how she would use what she was learning; even when she was working at her computer she would exclaim from time to time that she couldn't wait to take this back to her classroom. "My kids will love it!" By all the usual rules of evaluation, the workshop was going well. My educational objective for my students (the teachers) was set as learning Logo and the principles of programming, and the class was making reasonably rapid progress in this direction—and showing enthusiasm as well.

Despite this, I had a nagging feeling that something was wrong. I couldn't put my finger on what it was until a slight commotion broke out in the workshop. One of the other participants apparently had the same misgivings as I did but more quickly diagnosed the problem. Losing patience with the expressions of enthusiasm she muttered, "Forget the [expletive] children!" The reaction of the others in the room was electric: Some were shocked and protested; one immediately responded with a supporting remark. I was at first taken aback and then realized that the outburst captured what had been troubling me. The discordant element had been a sense I couldn't yet articulate that the participants thought of themselves as teachers-in-training rather than as learners. Their awareness of being teachers was preventing them from giving themselves over fully to experiencing what they were doing as intellectually exciting and joyful in its own right, for what it could bring them as private individuals. The major obstacle in the way of teachers becoming learners is inhibition about learning.

After the incident I felt something like Joe's sense of liberation. I was freed from a nagging fear about what was wrong and from needily seeking security in the teachers' exclamations of delight. My freedom allowed me to look more closely at what the individuals were doing with their programming, and soon I noticed a striking difference in style. Some were constructing the houses by putting together clean geometric shapes, in the simplest case following the example I had used in *Mindstorms:* A "house" can be made by putting a triangle on top of a square. One of the participants seemed uncomfortable with these shapes. Perhaps they had bad associations with School math or perhaps her personality biased her toward fuzzier things. Whatever its origin, the discomfort led her to pick up an idea from someone else's failure to make a neat geometric pattern to represent a flower garden. It came out as a wiggly line that might have been a failed flower garden but was just the thing to turn into smoke rising from the chimney of the house. After a while all the houses had smoke in varying patterns.

One thing led to another. The smoky effect could be adapted to draw clouds floating over the village and, with a little more adaptation, to draw trees and other less square objects than houses. Sometimes very small actions by a teacher can seed growth in a class. One that became important in this workshop was naming the emerging programming style. I dubbed it "smoky programming" and contrasted it with "hard-edged" programming.

The immediate effect was to encourage the original smoke maker. At this point it was an individual act involving teacher (myself) and student. Gradually it turned into something more social. Naming styles became a habit and encouraged personal pride in them; they became something to discuss and something to own. A vocabulary developed for talking about them, a sense of values for respecting others' styles even while taking pride in one's own.

In short, a process was under way that I would call the beginnings of a microculture. Talking about styles is an excellent seed for the development of a learning culture; it contributes to the richness of the immediate learning but also allows the benefits to flow into other areas, since styles can be recognized across a variety of different contents and activities. All learning benefits from talking about it—so long as the talk is good—and comparing styles is one of the best conversation starters provided that the differences are clear and the participants authentically respect the styles of others while defending their own. But for the talking to be good it must be both rooted in the real concerns of the participants and supported by knowledge and experience.

The issue of the contrast between the smoky and the hard-edged styles of programming was indeed very well rooted. It was not just a simple difference of style, though I was trying to promote a culture in which any difference would in fact be respected; on the contrary, the issue has been central in debates about alternative epistemologies. The hard-edged style is closer to the analytic, generalizable ways of thinking valued by the traditional "canonical" epistemology, which has come under fire from feminists as androcentric, from Afrocentrists as Eurocentric, and generally from many on the political left as representing the thinking of dominating groups. Indeed, research by MIT sociologist Sherry Turkle and myself shows that it is more likely to be the preferred style of white males. This is enough to make it very relevant to teachers, but in fact there is another aspect that makes it even more directly so. Moving from the hard-edged to the smoky style involved a step away from an abstract and formal approach to one that invites all the words that Piaget (taken as representative here of a far wider span of psychological thinking) would attach to the thinking of younger children: concrete, figural, animistic, and even egocentric.

Thus the issue is rooted in the teacher's concern about what kind of thinking is appropriate for children—but in such a complex way as to lend great importance to the second criterion for good talk about learning: the necessary knowledge and experience. Much more than "training" is needed for teachers to develop the ability to benefit from the presence of computers and to bring this benefit to their students.

It is instructive to note how a small Central American country has been able to handle this problem in a way that puts most

North American school systems to shame. I would suggest that this is largely because the country classified itself as a "developing country" and made this an advantage compared with countries that see themselves as "developed"—and so presumably have nowhere further to go. One moral of the story is that we might all do better if we dared classify ourselves as "developing."

In 1986 Oscar Arias was running for election as president of Costa Rica. The same mentality that would enable him to win the election, launch the peace process in Central America, and gain the Nobel prize was reflected in an election promise to take steps toward ensuring that Costa Rican children think of themselves as belonging to the modern world and not as Third World outsiders looking on longingly. One of his steps would be to bring computers into all the elementary schools of the country. Later I shall have several occasions to refer to aspects of what turned into a project with many exemplary features. Here I focus only on how the project did more than "train" its teachers.

For better or for worse, a decision was taken to invite corporations to submit complete plans, not only to supply and maintain computers but to determine the educational content, teacher preparation, and the evaluation process. This was a commercial plum involving many thousands of computers, so it was not surprising that fourteen companies submitted bids. IBM brought me in as a consultant and followed my advice to submit a plan that was exceptional in the proportion of effort devoted to the preparation of teachers in advance and their support during the project. This may not have seemed to make sense in terms of trimming prices in a competitive bid; but at the head of IBM's Latin American Education group was an energetic, intelligent, and not at all bureaucratic woman. Alejandrina Fernández persuaded her superiors in the corporation that IBM could afford to lose money in the first year of this project. It turned out that paying attention to the role of teachers won her the contract and has led to a successful model that has been used in half a dozen Latin American countries.

The Costa Rican government created a foundation to oversee

the project—an unusual case of a government having the wit to protect a project from its own bureaucracy! Within the foundation the discussion centered on the role of teachers. One group argued that the mode of use should be as easy on the teacher as possible. Many of the teachers in the rural districts had very little experience with technology and no formal education in anything technical. These teachers, it was argued, would be excluded by any mode of using the computers that required technical skills. Thus this group argued for using CAI software, and had this side won the contract would probably have gone to a company offering the kind of ("teacher-proof") turnkey system where the computer is switched on and the teacher doesn't even have to load a diskette—everything is automatically done under central control. The argument of the other group, though they did not quite put it in these words, was to make it as hard as possible for the teachers. In the end Costa Rica, under the leadership of Clotilda Fonseca, has mounted an exemplary program in which hundreds of teachers, most of whom indeed had no technical background, learned to program in Logo and derived a great new sense of confidence in themselves and their country by mastering something that was experienced as challenging, modern, difficult, and "not for people like them." This is in quite remarkable contrast with the position adopted by many American school districts that Logo is "educationally good" but "too hard for teachers"!

The debate was settled by an experiment in which a group of teachers participated in an intensive three-week Logo workshop. Although there is no objective way to make such measurements, I think it was obvious to all observers that an exceptional quantity of learning took place in these weeks. I think it was almost as obvious that this happened because the participating teachers felt that much more was involved than a technical improvement in learning basic skills. They were making a personal assertion of their will to appropriate this modern thing; a professional assertion against a view of teaching as a lowly profession; and a national assertion against the view of their country as underdeveloped. Many of them were also making an assertion of gender; for a large percentage of elementary school teachers are women and the organizers of the project had had the good sense to reflect this in the selection process.

The Costa Rica project showed in a specially clear form the computer playing a role in identity formation by teachers and brings us back full circle to the issue of negative representations of teachers. In a conversation with Oscar Arias, who asked me what I thought was the most interesting aspect of the project, I focused on what I have been saying here about teachers. Amazement and delight were written all over his face when he heard me talk about how much effort teachers had put into the project. He explained that what he had heard about teachers in the past was on the lines that they wanted more money for less work, and told me how pleased he was that his computer project had educated him as well. I left the presidential palace feeling proud to have been part of an opportunity for teachers to show themselves for what they are and to become a little more.

In addition to allowing teachers the opportunity to make the project part of a developing sense of identity, the *Programa Informatica Educativa* has another feature that makes it developmental for teachers. This is a compromise between the idea of a computer lab (which was imposed by financial constraints) and the classroom computer. The students do go to a separate room where the computers are located, but their regular classroom teacher goes with them. Moreover, the teacher learns with them, too, for in the lab there is also a computer teacher who has had an opportunity for development (to a degree that is rare even in the most "developed" countries) not only as a technical expert but also as the interpreter of a culture of learning.

Another version of the compromise had been the goal of a model pioneered by my MIT research group, first at the Lamplighter School in Dallas and then in Project Headlight at the Hennigan School in Boston. The model, which needed more resources than Costa Rica had been able to afford—though far less in proportion to the national wealth of the two countries—originally incorporated three essential principles. First, the number of computers would be sufficient for every class to spend at least one period each day with its regular teacher, when every student could have full access to a computer. Second, although any educational software might be used on occasion, the primary use of the computers would be based on the assumption that everyone, students and teachers, would be able to program the computer in Logo from the outset. Third, all the teachers would have not only sufficient expertise but also sufficient freedom of choice to use the computers in a manner that would express their personal styles of work. Later, a fourth principle grew out of these three when the Gardner Academy, a largely Latino inner-city elementary school in San Jose, developed its own implementation of the three principles under the name Project Mindstorm. This fourth principle asserts the advantage of the explicit development from within the school of a unique indigenous learning culture and philosophy of education. The project's name marked an intention to adopt my ideas; its divergence from what I had described myself was, in my view, part of a confirmation that it had succeeded. In education, the highest mark of success is not having imitators but inspiring others to do something else.

The project was created by the Technology Center of Silicon Valley, which let the project evolve without interference after it had selected a school and a director. The director was Carol Sperry, who came to computers after many years as a classroom teacher. I believe her own experience helped to empower the teachers in the project to create a culture in the school and to see it as *theirs*. She was not someone who came from a university or a school bureaucracy to tell teachers what to do with computers. Because she was a teacher herself, and did not feel answerable to anyone outside the school, she could ask the other teachers to join her in "putting herself in the disk drive along with the Logo disk." The intensity of the personal involvement created an unusually strong culture of teachers, and this in turn gave several of the teachers the intellectual confidence needed to nurture an unusual culture among students. An example will illustrate the point.

When I was discussing Brian and Henry, I quoted a student who talked about putting "grace" into his computer graphics. The student, who was from Project Mindstorm, explained that he wanted to grow up to put art and mathematics together. What is unusual here is not the fact that a student would say this, but rather that the teachers could cope with this way of thinking about mathematics. The special demand on the teacher is seen in another light: As long as there is a fixed curriculum, a teacher has no need to become involved in the question of what is and what is not mathematics. But here the teacher was willing to take on what would be considered a philosopher's question, and to become involved in serious discussion with students and with colleagues about whether this student's activities—which looked very different from *any* math in the curriculum, as the figures on page 80 show—were nevertheless mathematics.

In this chapter my thinking has been conceptual: I have presented a concept of School, a concept of the teacher, a concept of the bureaucrat, and a concept of struggle. I conclude here with some more pragmatic remarks on strategy for change.

What can be done to mobilize the potential force for change inherent in the position of teachers? First I must make some qualifications. The conflict I have described is one of idealized principle. In order to bring out the ideas, it comes too close to presenting an image of pure angels engaged in a holy war with evil demons. Real teachers have mixed positions. Everyone who has grown up in our society has internalized something of School's way and teachers are no exception. At the same time, most school administrators were once teachers and continue to share some of their yearnings. Hechinger's story is not about a wicked principal; it is about the *role* of principal: the office, not the person. Carol Sperry has written about "contradictions" even in teachers who think of themselves as militantly working for

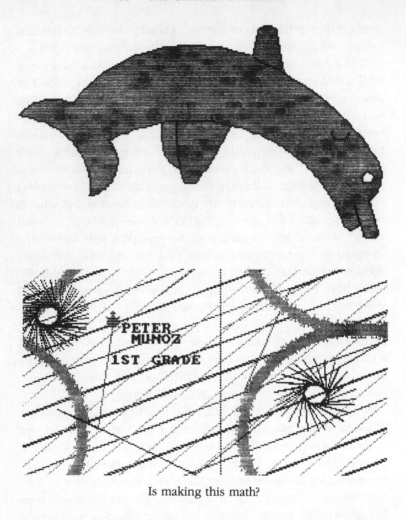

Is making this math?

change. From a feminist stance she sees women as the essential agents of change in education; but the same women have themselves internalized a model of women in a nonaggressive role of accepting authority and as teachers doubly so. The result is that when they try to implement change they often undo in subtle ways with the left hand what they have wrought with the right, often undermining their own view of things by their use of such language as, "I am just a teacher, but. . . ."

In brief, we are dealing with a situation of uneven development. The problem for society is to give teachers the same pluralist support that the best of them give their students. Individuals at different places need support to move from where they are. They cannot be cajoled or ordered into a too distant place. In my writing I hold out the image of an ideal; but even adopting the ideal fully is meaningless unless one can see the next small step. The practical consequence is that change cannot come about except pluralistically.

The central practical problem is to find ways in which teachers who are at different places in the willingness to work for change can do so. There cannot be a uniform change across the board—any attempt to do that will reduce the pace of change to that of the least common denominator. Society cannot afford to keep back its potentially best teachers simply because some, or even most, are unwilling.

5

• • •

A Word for Learning

WHY is there no word in English for the art of learning? Webster says that the word *pedagogy* means the art of teaching. What is missing is the parallel word for learning. In schools of education, courses on the art of teaching are often listed simply as "methods." Everyone understands that the methods of importance in education are those of teaching—these courses supply what is thought to be needed to become a skilled teacher. But what about methods of learning? What courses are offered for those who want to become skilled learners? The same imbalance can be found in words for the theories behind these two arts. "Theory of Instruction" and "Instructional Design" are among many ways of designating an academic area of study and research in support of the art of teaching. There are no similar designations for academic areas in support of the art of learning. Understandably: The need for such names has not been felt because there is so little to which they would apply. Pedagogy, the art of teaching, under its various names, has been adopted by the academic world as a respectable and an important field. The art of learning is an academic orphan.

One should not be misled by the fact that libraries of academic departments of psychology often have a section marked "learning theory." The older books under this heading deal with the activity that is sometimes caricatured by the image of a white-coated scientist watching a rat run through a maze; newer volumes are more likely to base their theories on the performance of computer programs than on the behavior of animals. I do not mean to denigrate such books—I am myself the coauthor of one and proud of it—but only to observe that they are not about the art of learning. They do not, for instance, offer advice to the rat (or the computer) about how to learn, though they have much to say to the psychologist about how to train a rat. Sometimes they are taken as a basis for training children, but I have not been able to find in them any useful advice about how to improve my own learning.

The unequal treatment by our language of the arts of learning and of teaching is visible in grammar as well as in vocabulary. Think, for example, of parsing the sentence, The teacher teaches a child. *Teacher* is the active subject of the sentence; *child* is the passive object. The teacher does something to the learner. This grammatical form bears the stamp of School's hierarchical ideology in representing teaching as the active process. The teacher is in control and is therefore the one who needs skill; the learner simply has to obey instructions. This asymmetry is so deeply rooted that even the advocates of "active" or "constructivist" education find it hard to escape. There are many books and courses on the art of constructivist teaching, which talk about the art of setting up situations in which the learner will "construct knowledge"; but I do not know any books on what I would assume to be the more difficult art of actually constructing the knowledge. The how-to-do-it literature in the constructivist subculture is almost as strongly biased to the teacher side as it is in the instructionist subculture.

A first step toward remedying these deficiencies is to give the missing area of study a name so that we can talk about it. Besides, it is only respectful to do this: Any culture that shows proper respect to the art of learning would have a name for it. In *Mindstorms* I proposed a word that did not catch on, but since I believe that there is more cultural readiness for such a word today I shall try again—always bearing in mind that my principal goal is less to advocate this particular word than to emphasize the need for one. If the culture is really ripe for such a word, many people will throw in their own words (perhaps simply by quietly using them) and eventually one will take root in the soil of the language. Linnaeus, the father of botanical terminology, could decide to call a familiar white flower *Bellis perennis,* but the common language calls it a daisy, ignoring the Latin name as it ignores the botanist's insistence that a daisy is an "inflorescence" and not a flower at all. A person can propose; "the culture" or "the language" disposes.

In any case, to illustrate the gap in our language and my proposal for filling it, consider the following sentence: When I learned French I acquired ———— knowledge about the language, ———— knowledge about the people, and ———— knowledge about learning. *Linguistic* and *cultural* would fill in the first two blanks with no problems; but the reader will be hard put to think up a word to fill in the third blank. My candidate is *mathetic,* and I thereby make restitution for a semantic theft perpetrated by my professional ancestors, who stole the word *mathematics* from a family of Greek words related to learning. *Mathēmatikos* meant "disposed to learn," *mathēma* was "a lesson," and *manthanein* was the verb "to learn." Mathematicians were so convinced that theirs was the only true learning that they felt justified in appropriating the word, and succeeded so well that the dominant connotation of the stem *math-* is now that stuff about numbers they teach in School. One of the few traces of the original sense of the root retained by current English is "polymath." This isn't a person who knows many kinds of mathematics, but one who has learned broadly. Following my proposal, I would use the noun *mathetics* for a course on the art of learning, as in: "Mathetics (by whatever name it will come to be known) is even more important than mathematics as an area of study for children."

A comparison with another Greek borrowing for talking about mental process will clarify the intended meaning of "mathetics" and perhaps support its "sound" and "feel." *Heuristics*—from the same stem as Archimedes' cry "Eureka!"—means the art of intellectual discovery. In recent times it has been applied specifically to discovering solutions of problems. Thus mathetics is to learning what heuristics is to problem solving.

Although the idea of heuristics is old—it goes back at least to Descartes and, if one stretches it a little, to the Greeks—its influence on contemporary educational thinking is mainly due to mathematician George Polya, who is best known through his book *How to Solve It*. His theme runs parallel to my complaint that School gives more importance to knowledge about numbers and grammar than to knowledge about learning, except that in place of the word *learning*, Polya says "principles of solving problems." I would echo this wholeheartedly: In school children are taught more about numbers and grammar than about thinking. In an early paper (1972) that supported and extended Polya's ideas, I even formulated this as a challenging paradox:

> It is usually considered good practice to give people instruction in their occupational activities. Now, the occupational activities of children are learning, thinking, playing, and the like. Yet, we tell them nothing about those things. Instead, we tell them about numbers, grammar, and the French Revolution; somehow hoping that from this disorder the really important things will emerge all by themselves. And they sometimes do. But the alienation-dropout-drug complex is certainly not less frequent. . . . The paradox remains: why don't we teach them to think, to learn, to play?

Traditional education sees intelligence as inherent in the human mind and therefore in no need of being learned. This would mean that it is proper for School to teach facts, ideas, and values on the assumption that human beings (of any age) are endowed by nature with the ability to use them. Polya's challenge started with the simple observation that students' ability to solve problems improved when he instructed them to follow such simple rules as: Before doing anything else, spend a little time trying to think of other problems that are similar to the one in hand. He went on to develop a collection of other "heuristic" rules in the same spirit, some of which, like this one, apply to all kinds of problems and some to specific areas of knowledge, among which Polya himself paid most attention to mathematics.

Another typical example of Polya's type of rule adapts the principle of "divide and conquer." Students often fail to solve a problem because they insist on trying to solve the whole problem all at once; in many cases they would have an easier time of it if they were to recognize that parts of the problem can be solved separately and later put together to deal with the whole. Thus the Wright Brothers had the intention from the beginning of building a powered airplane that could take off from a field, but had they tried to build such a thing for their first experiments they would very likely have come to the same gory end as many of their predecessors. Instead they solved the problem of wing design by inventing and building a wind tunnel in which they tested wing sections. Then they built a glider that would take off from a track lined up with the wind in a place where winds were ideal. Independently of all this they also worked on an engine. In this way they gradually conquered the problems.

Polya wished to introduce into education a more explicit treatment of the principles of what is often called "problem solving." In the same way, I want to introduce a more explicit treatment of the principles of learning. But thinking about heuristics helps explain the idea of mathetics in another way as well. By offering my own unorthodox explanation of why heuristic principles help students, I shall try to bring out a contrast between *heuristics* and *mathetics.*

I believe that problem solving uses processes far more subtle than those captured in Polya's rules. This is not to say that the rules are not valuable as aids to solving problems, but I do think that their most important role is less direct and much simpler than their literal meaning. Attempting to apply heuristic rules checks students in the rush to get done with a problem and get on with the next. It has them spend more time with the problems, and my mathetic point is simply that spending relaxed time with a problem leads to getting to know it, and through this, to improving one's ability to deal with other problems like it. It is not using the rule that solves the problem; it is thinking about the problem that fosters learning. So does talking about the problems or showing them to someone else. What is mathetic here is the shift of focus from thinking about whether the rules themselves are effective in the immediate application to looking for multiple explanations of how working with the rules can contribute in the longer run to learning. To make the point in a possibly exaggerated form, I suggest that any kind of "playing with problems" will enhance the abilities that lie behind their solution.

This interpretation of why heuristic methods work highlights several mathetically important themes, each of which points to a way in which School impedes learning and to some good advice about how to do it better.

To begin with, the theme of "taking time," just mentioned in connection with Polya, is well illustrated by a passage from a book whose name has more than once raised eyebrows when I quoted it in academic circles: the best-selling *The Road Less Traveled,* by psychiatrist M. Scott Peck. I read the book in the first place for the same reason that I have made alliances with Lego and Nintendo, which has also caused some academically pure and politically correct eyebrows to rise at the idea of having any connection with people who make money. Anyone who can draw as many people into situations related to learning as Peck, Lego, or Nintendo knows something that educators who have trouble holding the attention of thirty children for forty minutes ought to want to learn.

Here is what Peck has to say about taking time:

At the age of thirty-seven I learned how to fix things. Prior to that time almost all my attempts to make minor plumbing repairs, mend toys or assemble boxed furniture according to the accompanying hieroglyphical instruction sheet ended in confusion, failure and frustration. Despite having managed to make it through medical school and support a family as a more or less successful executive and psychiatrist, I considered myself to be a mechanical idiot. I was convinced I was deficient in some gene, or by curse of nature lacking some mystical quality responsible for mechanical ability. Then one day at the end of my thirty-seventh year, while taking a spring Sunday walk, I happened upon a neighbor in the process of repairing a lawn mower. After greeting him I remarked, "Boy, I sure admire you. I've never been able to fix those kind of things or do anything like that." My neighbor, without a moment's hesitation, shot back, "That's because you don't take the time." I resumed my walk, somehow disquieted by the gurulike simplicity, spontaneity and definitiveness of his response. "You don't suppose he could be right, do you?" I asked myself. Somehow it registered, and the next time the opportunity presented itself to make a minor repair I was able to remind myself to take my time. The parking brake was stuck on a patient's car, and she knew that there was something one could do under the dashboard to release it, but she didn't know what. I lay down on the floor below the front seat of her car. Then I took the time to make myself comfortable. Once I was comfortable, I then took the time to look at the situation. I looked for several minutes. At first all I saw was a confusing jumble of wires and tubes and rods, whose meaning I did not know. But gradually, in no hurry, I was able to focus my sight on the brake apparatus and trace its course. And then it became clear to me that there was a little latch preventing the brake from being released. I slowly studied this latch until it became clear to me that if I were to push it upward with the tip of my finger it would move easily and would release the brake. And so I did this. One single motion, one ounce of pressure from a fingertip, and the problem was solved. I was a master mechanic!

Actually, I don't begin to have the knowledge or the time to gain that knowledge to be able to fix most mechanical failures, given the fact that I choose to concentrate my time on non-mechanical matters. So I still usually go running to the nearest repairman. But I now know that this is a choice I make, and I am not cursed or genetically defective or otherwise incapacitated or impotent. And I know that I and anyone else who is not mentally defective can solve any problem if we are willing to take the time.

Give yourself time is an absurdly obvious principle that falls equally under heuristics and mathetics. Yet School flagrantly contravenes it by its ways of chopping time: "Get out your books . . . do ten problems at the end of chapter 18 . . . DONG . . . there's the bell, close the books." Imagine a business executive, or a brain surgeon, or a scientist who had to work to such a fragmented schedule.

This story speaks as poignantly about a second theme—talking—as about time. Peck does not say this explicitly, but one can guess that he would have had the epiphany about taking his time at an earlier age than thirty-seven had he talked more often to more people about his and their experiences with mechanical problems. A central tenet of mathetics is that good discussion promotes learning, and one of its central research goals is to elucidate the kinds of discussion that do most good and the kinds of circumstances that favor such discussions. Yet in most circles talking about what really goes on in our minds is blocked by taboos as firm as those that inhibited Victorians from expressing their sexual fantasies. These taboos are encouraged by School, but go far beyond it, and point to ways in which our general culture is profoundly "antimathetic."

An extreme example will vividly illustrate the antimathetic process that exists in many more subtle, but destructive, forms in School. The incident took place in a "resource room," where children diagnosed as having a learning disability spend part of their day. Third-grader Frank was one of them.

An aide gave Frank a set of sums to do on a piece of paper. I knew the child bitterly hated doing sums on paper, although under other conditions he could work quite successfully with numbers. For example, I had seen him do quite impressive calculations of how many and what shapes of Lego pieces he needed for a job he wanted to do. To deal with the school demand to calculate with numbers in isolation from real needs, he had a number of techniques. One was to use his fingers, but his teacher had observed this and ruled that it was not allowed. As he sat in the resource room I could see him itching to do finger manipulations. But he knew better. Then I saw him look around for something else to count with. Nothing was at hand. I could see his frustration grow. What could I do? I could pull rank and persuade the aide to give him something else to do or allow finger counting. But this wouldn't solve any real problems: Tomorrow he'd be back in the same situation. Educate the aide? This wasn't the time or place. Inspiration came! I walked casually up to the boy and said out loud: "Did you think about your teeth?" I knew instantly from his face that he got the point, and from the aide's face that she didn't. "Learning disability indeed!" I said to myself. He did his sums with a half-concealed smile, obviously delighted with the subversive idea.

In a classic joke, a child stays behind after school to ask a personal question. "Teacher, what did I learn today?" The surprised teacher asks, "Why do you ask that?" and the child replies, "Daddy always asks me and I never know what to say."

What did Frank learn at school that day? If asked, the aide might have said that he did ten addition problems and so learned about adding. What would Frank say? One thing that is certain is that he would be very unlikely to speak to his teacher about his newly found trick for turning tongue and teeth into an abacus. Despite his learning disability, he had long before learned not to talk too much about what was really happening in his head. He has already encountered too many teachers who demanded not only that he get the right answer but also that he get it in the way they have decreed. Learning to let them think that he was doing it their way was part of belonging to the culture of School.

Frank's might be an extreme case, but most people share a similar fear of being made vulnerable by exposing themselves as having an inferior or messy mind. From this fear grows a habit that almost has the force of a taboo against talking freely about how we think and most especially about how we learn. If so, my joke with Frank fits very well with Freud's theory that jokes are funny precisely because they aren't—they express repressed feelings that are not funny at all, in this case an undertone of something wrong with School's way of talking (and especially its way of not talking) about learning. Freud was thinking of jokes relieving tensions that come from hiding aggressivity and living with taboos on sexual instincts. I believe there is a similar situation in relation to learning.

This mathetic taboo has much in common with the taboos that existed until recently against talking about sexual matters. In Victorian days, or even when I was a child, sexual fantasies fell under the concept of "dirty thoughts," and although it was acceptable to recognize that other people had them, respectable people did not speak aloud about their own. It is relevant here to speculate about what lay behind this reluctance to talk. Imagine that you are a Victorian. Now, while you might be pretty sure that you are not the only one who has dirty thoughts, you would not know just how common it is, or whether people would assume you do. So better keep your mouth shut.

Whether or not this is an accurate account of Victorian sex taboos, I am sure that something analogous happens nowadays. Today, few people worry about letting on that their minds are full of sexual thoughts; many even feel a taboo against *not* talking in public about this topic. Contemporary taboos bear on different aspects of the mind. The most relevant here of many such restraints on intimacy shows itself as a widespread reluctance to allow others to see how much confusion pervades one's thinking.

We do not like to appear "ignorant" or "stupid" or just plain wrong. Of course, we all know that our own minds are full of messy confusion and that many others are in the same plight; but we imagine that some minds are tidy and neat and sharp and see no reason to advertise not being in this class, especially in the presence of people such as bosses and teachers who have power over us. So voices within caution us to be careful of what we say: Talking too much might reveal what kind of mind we have, and make us vulnerable. Eventually this caution becomes a habit.

The analogy with sexual taboos may seem to exaggerate the reluctance to talk freely about personal learning. I doubt it. My own struggle to achieve what degree of liberation I have in this respect has given me a sense of a very strong taboo. Even now, although I have a relatively good base of intellectual security, I often catch myself in the act of covering over the confusion in my mind. I can't seem to help wanting to give certain people an impression of greater clarity than I have and, indeed, than I think anyone really has. I have developed—and I cannot believe that I am alone in this—a whole battery of defense mechanisms, as will shortly be seen.

Exaggerated or not, the suggestion of a taboo is intended to state emphatically that getting people to talk about learning is not simply a matter of providing the subject matter and the language. The lack of language is important. But there is also an active resistance of some kind. Thus advancing toward the goal of mathetics requires more than technical aids to discussion. It also requires developing a system of psychological support.

The simplest form of support system I can imagine is to adopt the practice of opening oneself by freely talking about learning experiences. The rest of this chapter presents an example by describing how I myself emerged from what I believe it is appropriate to call a learning disability, which afflicted me for nearly twice as long as Peck's sense of himself as a mechanical idiot.

A child at school who fails to read or do arithmetic at the appropriate age is likely to be diagnosed as suffering from a learning disability and placed in special classes. I was able to read and add at the usual age, but there were other areas where my learning fell far behind what some children did at my age. Peck reports that he discovered when he was thirty-seven that he could, after all, deal with mechanical problems. It took me a longer time to recover from a learning disability that had plagued me as long as I can remember: I could not remember the names of flowers. Admittedly, my agnosia in this domain was not complete. As long as I can remember I could correctly apply the words *rose, tulip,* and *daffodil* to the common varieties of these plants. But I cannot really say that I knew what a rose was. I was repeatedly in embarrassing situations; when I admired the roses in a garden, they would turn out to be camellias or even tulips. I certainly did not recognize wild species as roses. The names *chrysanthemum, dahlia, marigold,* and *carnation* formed a blurry cloud in my mind. The extent of my not knowing is illustrated by an incident that happened well into the transition to "flower literacy" that I shall be chronicling in the following pages.

A pot of plants with rather showy blooms appeared in a common space in the building where I have my office. At the time I was beginning to pay attention to flowers and was delighted by what appeared to me to be a very exotic specimen. When I tried to remember whether I had seen one before, the only thought that came to mind was that it wasn't a morning glory (a species I had "discovered" in the previous weeks). As often happens to people with learning disabilities, a strong feeling of discomfort inhibited me from simply asking the name of the plant. Instead, I tried to strike up conversations about the plant's beauty, hoping that someone would mention the name in passing.

By the time I had failed four or five times, I was engrossed in the game of finding the name without actually asking. At this point I stopped to think, and came up with a better ploy than undirected conversation. Addressing someone who struck me as the kind of person who would know about flowers, I said: "Isn't that an unusual variety?" and success came in the form of: "Oh, I don't really know one variety of petunia from another." Petunia! In the next few weeks I noticed petunias twenty times before I stopped counting. I don't imagine that some person or destiny was planting them in my path. In summer in New England, petunias are everywhere. The real puzzle is how I could have been blind to them all those years. How was it possible that so many people around me had always known what a petunia looked like while I didn't? What was wrong with me?

I don't think anything is "wrong with me," but even with all the intellectual security I have been able to build on the basis of academic successes, I am still vulnerable to doubts about myself. The pain occasioned by my doubts makes me wonder about the feelings of children who find it so much more difficult than their comrades to learn to read or to add. Although the consequences of my disability were so much milder than theirs that any comparison risks being condescending, I do think there are enough common elements to make the comparison valuable. At the very least my failure to benefit from Schoolish remedies gives reason to think more carefully about standard approaches to "special education."

In School's discourse the idea of motivation plays a primary role. "If kids won't learn they must be unmotivated, so let's motivate them." The advice certainly has no direct application to my case, for in every simple sense of the word I was already highly motivated. I often made resolutions to conquer my flower disability, and these would lead to a spurt of intense flower name-learning activity. For the same reason, laziness is no explanation either. We have to look more deeply for much more subtle and textured notions for thinking about these disabilities and strategies to overcome them. For example, in the place of the one-dimensional concept of "being motivated," I shall develop a concept of relationship with areas of knowledge having all the complexity and nuance of relationships with people.

I find it significant that despite all my fancy ideas about learning, I would fall back on Schoolish modes of learning flower names. Looking for a teacher, I'd go into a flower shop and ask:

What are those? And those? And those? Looking for a textbook, I bought a book from which I tried to associate photographs of flowers with their names. I even went on field trips to the botanical gardens where I would peer at the name tags of all the flowers. But to no avail. The frontal attack by rote learning didn't work any better for me than the same Schoolish methods do for children who have trouble learning School's subjects. It was like learning for a school test. I'd remember the names of a few flowers for a while, but they would soon sink back into the familiar confusion. After a while the paroxysm of flower learning would pass, and I'd resign myself for another year or two to being someone who "isn't good at" flower names.

One day a break came serendipitously. I was in the country in the late spring among people who were talking about how wonderful the lupines were doing. Feeling excluded and not wanting to admit in that particular company that I had no idea what a lupine was, I used the trick that later served me well in the petunia situation. I said: "Isn't *Loo Pin* a strange name? I wonder what its origin could possibly be?" (Getting a conversation going is a good ploy used cunningly by many "learning-disabled" children.) Someone speculated intelligently: "Sounds like Wolf—lupus the wolf. But I don't see the connection." After a few rounds of comment in scattered directions (which would have died out if I hadn't kept stoking the conversational fire), someone said: "It looks like a wolf's tail." Someone grumbled that it didn't really. That's a relative judgment, for what mattered to me was that of all the plants in sight, only one could possibly be perceived as being in the slightest like a wolf's tail. So I concluded, correctly, that those colorful masses of what I have since learned to describe as "tall spikes" were lupines.

The aspect of the serendipity that played a key role in my development wasn't discovering what those flowers were called; it wasn't making a connection between a flower and a name. It was making a connection between two areas of knowledge: flower names and a particular kind of interest I happen to have in etymology. Previous experience leads me to expect that I would soon have forgotten the name *lupine,* but this time I was so delighted at my cleverness and intrigued by the etymological puzzle that the incident was still buzzing in my head when I got back to my books and could explore the word. I read that *lupine* does indeed derive from the Latin word for "wolf," but not because of the tail-like appearance of its spike. The word is traced to a belief that lupines were bad for the soil because they "wolfed" all the nutrients. Enjoyment of the wolf-theory's ambiguous status between true and false led me to pursue the research and run into a twist in the story that made it still more evocative for me.

As long as I can remember, I have been excited by paradoxical aspects of words, and so my level of excitement rose when I found a paradoxical slant to the etymology of *lupine.* One no longer thinks of the lupine as wolfing nutrients; on the contrary, the lupine, as a member of the pea family, is able to capture nitrogen from the atmosphere and add value to the soil. Seeing them in poor soil is cause for praise rather than blame. But the name outlived the theory on which it was based, and so became one of many examples of old ideas that are preserved in our language and maintain connections of which we are only marginally aware. My relationship with flower names was taking on a new tone as they made contact with areas I found personally interesting.

This twist also touched on another personally evocative issue. One reason for my fondness for etymology is that it provides good examples for a vendetta against the idea of any single explanation of mental phenomena. They are *all* multiply determined—and this is the essence of the way the mind works. Now the origins of flower names began to show promise as an area in which I could find strong but very simple support for this way of thinking. At first blush etymology may seem to run counter to my preference for multiple explanations, since it so often seems to pinpoint a single historical source for a word. But finding a source is not a psychological or cultural explanation of the way the word is used. The wolfing-of-goodness theory may be at the root of a full explanation of old popular forms that seem to have been followed by Linnaeus when he called this genus of plants *Lupinus,* but it scarcely begins to be an explanation of why the name has stuck in our culture. Explaining why botanists call a plant what they do does not explain why plain folk do so—in most cases the popular language scorns the botanical name and develops its own. We say *lilac* rather than *syringa* and wear a *carnation* rather than a *dianthus* in a buttonhole. It seems plausible that a folk etymology such as the looks-like-a-wolf's-tail theory could have contributed together with the wolfing-the-goodness theory to making the name *lupine* stick in popular usage. After all, if the association occurred to one person, it is reasonable to assume that it occurred to others and that it hovers near the threshold of consciousness of many more.

My mathetic theory does not depend on the truth of my amateur etymologizing. What matters here is that it was connected with regions of knowledge that were strongly evocative for me. The real moral of the story is how a certain engaging quality spread from words to flowers, and later from flowers to other mental domains. If I had to sum it up in a single metaphor, I would say it is about how "cold" mental regions were heated up through contact with "hot" regions.

One contact was not enough to heat up the previously chilly region of flower names. By now, as I write two years after the lupine incident, there has been dramatic change in my memory for flower names. It is as if they now find a place to stick. But this did not happen all at once, and by the time it did, much more than the ability to remember their names had changed in my relationship with plants.

For most of a year there was not much change, although I did not forget the word *lupine* and I did notice myself paying attention to oddities in flower names. For example, I caught myself playing with the minor contradictions suggested by an etymologically literal-minded hearing of "white lilac" or "yellow rose." *Lilac* derives from a Persian word for the color lilac, and rosy cheeks never suggest jaundice or pallor. One can tune one's ear to sense the same kind of oddness in hearing that water lilies and arum lilies aren't (in a botanical sense) lilies at all. Sometimes I felt impatient with myself for paying attention to such trivial thoughts, but they kept making small ripples in my mind, and in retrospect I am glad because these ripples put me in a state of readiness for the grand whammer. One night (reading at about two in the morning) I ran headlong into the fact that for a botanist a daisy is not a flower.

I can't tell whether I was more shocked at this being so or at my having lived so long without knowing it. A daisy not a flower? Come on! It's the prototypical flower—if you had asked me last year to draw a flower, I'm sure I'd have produced something more like a daisy than like anything else. Though it seems silly now, and rather ignorant, I really was upset and excited. I ran from book to book in the small hours, trying to learn more. The news was bad: The putsch against standard nomenclature went beyond daisies to include sunflowers and black-eyed susans and chrysanthemums and dahlias. They were denigrated with names like "false flower" or elevated with fancy names like "inflorescence," but it appeared that in many circles it is a definite gaffe to call them flowers. How can this be? A sunflower isn't a flower? Even arum lilies, which had already been slighted in my mind by not being lilies, were now excluded from being flowers.

The most powerful moment came in the morning when I could at last get hold of some flowers. I found myself in a situation that would be repeated several times in the following year: I was looking at a familiar object with a sense of looking at it for the first time. Compare a buttercup with a daisy and you may begin to understand how the botanist sees them as fundamentally different things. For the botanist a flower is structured around its sex organs: The stamens and anthers, the pistils, stigmas, and ovaries are the essence of the flower. The petals and sepals that make such a spectacularly colorful impression on us

The family of flowers that includes daisies, asters, sunflowers, and coneflowers are called inflorescences because what we usually call a flower is seen by the botanist as a mass of tiny flowers.

and on the birds and insects are secondary features. In the buttercup, the tulip, and the lily you can see all these parts—but not in the daisy. Or rather, in the daisy you see the parts repeated many times, for those white slivers you may have pulled off one by one while reciting "loves me . . . loves me not . . ." are not petals surrounding sex organs but entire flowers. If you pull one out very carefully, you will see that it is like a miniature, lopsided, and elongated petunia. And what they surround, the central yellow disk, is itself a mass of even tinier complete flowers. So botanically speaking, the daisy is not a flower but a tight bunch of flowers of two kinds, ray flowers on the outside surrounding disk flowers on the inside. The botanist will call it a head or an inflorescence, though I suppose and hope that children will always call it a flower.

The disk or mass at the center of many inflorescences is made up of many tiny flowers like this one. What seem to be petals are also complete flowers in themselves.

Up to this point my new involvement with flowers was confined to their names and belonged squarely in my established area of hot interest in etymology. With the daisy incident it broke out from words to things. I began to look at flowers and think about their structure. The concept of flower was changing, and new conceptual entities began to grow in my mind: The unit of thought shifted from the flower to the whole plant, and, by degrees, previously nebulous entities such as "the rose family" (which includes cherries, apples, and strawberries as well as roses) acquired firmer reality. I also began to think about botanists: It was easy to see that their definition of *flower* excluded daisies; this was a simple matter of logic. But coming to appreciate the reasons for adopting such a definition was an essentially different and more complex process, better characterized as entering a culture than as understanding a concept.

Naming remained an important theme in an increasingly complex set of relationships in my mind. A simple example started with the name of the daisy. Now that the humble flower had become such a center of interest, I naturally poked around the origins and meanings of its name. I could hardly believe my luck: *daisy* is "day's eye"! What a find, accompanied again by amazement at not having known this and even some shamefaced puzzling about why it hadn't been obvious. The find got extra spice from the fact that different books gave different explanations. One theory had the daisy looking like the sun, which is the "eye of the day"; another associated it with the tendency of daisies to open in the day and close at night. Another started with a speculation. I had run into the fact that daisies were thought to have good medicinal properties for afflictions of the eye. A first guess that this might be related to its name seemed to me too implausible to be worth checking. Doing so all the same led to another curious find: the doctrine of signatures, which held that plants show by their visible properties their medicinal virtues. The self-heal, a wildflower, shows its value for treating throat ailments by the fact that its flower has a throat, and this is reflected in the derivation of its botanical name, *Prunella vulgaris,* from *Breune,* the German word for "quinsy" (an old-fashioned name, as I learned through the same investigation, for tonsillitis). The coloration patterns of hepatica leaves are said to suggest the appearance of the liver, thus explaining both the name *hepatica*—from the Latin word meaning "having to do with the liver"—and the belief that it is good for liver ailments. Certain features of plants became more salient, for example, that some have throats and some don't. The interest in names was bringing me into the real world of flowers.

Other connections with names and naming led into new relationships with nature. The window of the room where most of this book was written looks out on a field in which I see wildflowers of several colors, particularly yellows and purples. Among the yellows I can see tall, bushy Saint-John's-worts and even taller evening primroses, little cinquefoils, and some early goldenrod. Among the purples I see fireweed, loosestrife, and asters. I also see some that are question marks in my head: I have noted their existence but don't know what they are. Two years ago I saw an undifferentiated display of pretty flowers. It was beautiful. I loved it. But it was not at all what I am seeing now. Try as I might I cannot make my eye go back to seeing it as I did before. I cannot imagine what it would be like to see those yellow flowers as a mass of yellow flowers without individual identity.

I want to pursue a detail in this development as a model for the process of learning. Two years ago I knew the name *buttercup* and correctly applied it to common buttercups. I cannot recall how widely I would have used this name to apply to other species, but I am sure that I had no other words for small yellow flowers. Early in the first summer I became aware of two other kinds of yellow wildflowers: cinquefoils and Saint-John's-worts. But my degree of flower dyslexia showed itself in the fact that I had to reidentify these flowers many times—like someone who cannot hold a tune, I could not hold the distinction from one day to the next. All the same, something had happened: It was as if I had made pegs in my head for three things—buttercups, cinquefoils, and Saint-John's-worts—but didn't yet know what to hang on each peg, or that I had met three people and had been told their names, but knew nothing else about them. I often find myself in this situation and am struck by how I get new entities mixed up until a gradually growing sense of individuality becomes strong enough to keep them separate. The sense of individuality grew slowly and unevenly for the three kinds of plant.

I do not pretend to know exactly how this process of growth happened. But I do know how it did not happen: I tried to memorize the characteristics of each group taken from a book, but this simply did not work. Perhaps if I had been interested only in these three flowers, I would have been able to memorize their formal characterizations. But if I turned to other plants and came back to the three yellow ones, I would get it wrong again. Slowly something different from rote memory of botanists' defining characteristics developed; I began to build up a more personal kind of connection.

I associate buttercups with folklore that tells about the appearance of a person's chin when a buttercup is held up to it. If the chin takes on the yellow color by reflection, this is interpreted in America as a sign of liking butter and in France, naturally, as a sign of being in love. Through these stories I associate the buttercup with shiny petals, one of the characteristics that in fact distinguishes it from the other two. Other associations were less direct. One of the three flowers has especially bushy stamens. I couldn't remember which. In fact, it is the Saint-John's-wort, but when I read that this plant is also known as Aaron's beard, I associated this name with bushy stamens because these are like a beard, and with the name Saint-John's-wort because Aaron and St. John both have a biblical connection. So the name Aaron's beard acted as a kind of glue to stick the bushy stamen property to the name *Saint-John's-wort*. During the same period I found my visual attention shifting from the flower to the plant, and this brought new kinds of association. And so it went.

The deeper I got into my "affair" with flowers, the more connections were made; and more connections meant that I was drawn in all the more strongly, that the new connections supported one another more effectively, and that they were more and more likely to be long-lasting. Moreover, the content of my learning spread in many directions: I was learning Latin words, I was picking up insights into the history of folk-medicine, and I was gaining or renewing geographic and historical knowledge. The Renaissance in its artistic and scientific aspects came into new focus through the role of flowers in the new relationship with nature that developed at that time.

My learning had hit a critical level, in the sense of the critical-mass phenomenon of a nuclear reaction or the explosion of a population when conditions favor both birthrate and survival. The simple moral is that learning explodes when you stay with it: A full year had passed before the effect in my mind reached a critical level for an exponential explosion of growth. The more complex moral is that some domains of knowledge, such as plants, are especially rich in connections and particularly prone to give rise to explosions of learning.

My learning experience with flowers began with a very narrow "curriculum": learning to name them. In the end the experience widened and left me a different person in more dimensions of life than anything that is measured by the standardized behavioristic tests with which the conservatives judge School learning. It affected my stream of consciousness as I moved about the world: I see more as I walk in the street or in a field. The world is more beautiful. My sense of oneness with nature is stronger. My caring about environmental issues is deep and more personal. And recently I have surprised myself by enjoying systematic books on botany and having no trouble remembering what I read. It is as if I have made my transition in this domain from a concrete to a formal stage.

Early in this chapter I mentioned a mathetic weakness in the literature on constructivism. The metaphor of learning by constructing one's own knowledge has great rhetorical power against the image of knowledge transmitted though a pipeline from teacher to student. But it is only a metaphor, and reflection on my flower story consolidates my sense that other images are just as useful for understanding learning, and are more useful as sources of practical mathetic guidance. One of these is *cultivation:* Developing my knowledge of plants felt more like the work of a horticulturalist designing, planting, and tending a garden than the work of a construction crew putting up a house. I have no doubt that my knowledge developed even when I was not paying attention! Another image is the geographic metaphor of regions and the idea of connections between them. Indeed, the description "connectionism" fits my story better than "constructivism."

On a pragmatic level, "Look for connections!" is sound mathetic advice, and on a theoretical level the metaphor leads to a range of interesting questions about the connectivity of knowledge. It even suggests that the deliberate part of learning consists of making connections between mental entities that already exist; new mental entities seem to come into existence in more subtle ways that escape conscious control. However that may be, thinking about the interconnectivity of knowledge suggests a theory of why some knowledge is so easily acquired without deliberate teaching. In the sense in which it is said that no two Americans are separated by more than five handshakes, this cultural knowledge is so interconnected that learning will spread by free migration to all its regions. This suggests a strategy to facilitate learning by improving the connectivity in the learning environment, by actions on cultures rather than on individuals.

6

• • •

An Anthology of
Learning Stories

THE word *anthology* will do to capture a key point about mathetics: the richness of connectivity of the things we know. In my case, the etymology of *lupine* led to new relationships with flowers, which in turn led me to acquire several hundred entirely new words and "heated up" my awareness of thousands of old friends. I must have known the word *anther* (the pollen sac of a flower's stamen), and its Greek stem *anthos,* meaning flower, from my school days. But I knew them "coldly." When they heated up they stirred connections, and I began to wonder whether *anthology* had an ancestral meaning of "studying flowers." This, however, turned out to be a false analogy with words like *biology.* Actually, the suffix *-logy* has a more general etymological sense than "study of." Its Greek (and Indo-European) stem meant "collect" before it meant "study," which could be regarded as collecting knowledge. Etymologically, *anthology* is a collection or bunch of flowers. Think of *trilogy,* which is not the study of threeness but a collection of three things.

This chapter is a collection of learning stories, each of which is prefaced and postfaced with just some of the learning morals that can be taken from it. The stories deal alternately with children using technology in a school and with people in the "real world."

Debbie Learns Fractions

In my discussion of my relationship with plants I suggested two modes of learning. Propositions cleanly state a well-delimited fact, such as "Potentilla is a genus in the rose family." Explorations establish a relatively messy web of connections which may link potentillas with buttercups and oenethera and etymologies and cabbages and kings. I probably gave the impression of strongly favoring the messy web over the clean proposition. I would stand by this insofar as the web can include the proposition, but the propositional does not include the web. Ideally, one should be able to draw on both and move fluently between them. But I should much rather have a messy intuitive understanding of something that I have not been able to formulate in a crisp proposition than have a crisp, clean proposition without an intuition to back it. Unfortunately, School's preference for the testable, delimitable, and listable proposition reverses this order. The result is isolated pieces of "knowledge" without the intuitions and the connections that would justify taking off those quote marks.

For three months Debbie and the other members of her fourth-grade class were engaged for an hour a day in a project that turned the tables on the use of the computer for automated instruction, generally known as CAI. Here the fourth-graders had the assignment of using Logo to develop a piece of instructional software to teach something about fractions; they became producers instead of consumers of educational software. To the true believer in CAI, this reversal will seem as perverse as telling people who need to move from point A to point B that they should build cars instead of using them. But the fact is that making the software did turn out to favor learning about fractions—as well, of course, as learning

Logo programming and other skills specifically related to making software. (I would not deduce that the same reversal applies to building cars, though it is far from impossible that building one might make a person a better driver!)

The paradox in the reversal is especially marked in the case of Debbie. The students were free to choose what they wanted their software to explain about fractions. Some of them chose to explain how to do the kinds of manipulation that come up in school tests—such as converting two-fourths to one-half. Debbie was one of those whose test scores showed significant improvement even though what she chose to explain was something more philosophical and far removed from any of the skills on which she would be tested. She formulated her philosophical principle in a number of ways, including, "You can use fractions every day of your life," and, "You can put fractions on everything." What she meant by these statements will become apparent from the context of her work.

In an interview early in the research project (which formed the core of a Ph.D. dissertation by my colleague and former student Idit Harel), the children were asked the simple question, "What's a fraction?" Their answers to this question were even more disquieting than their low test scores. Some seemed unable to give any sort of answer beyond an example, which was usually "a half." One said, "We haven't done that yet," evidently meaning not that they hadn't "done" fractions in class—of which, so far as these children were concerned, they had done plenty—but that they hadn't yet been told how to define a fraction. Many gave an answer that could be considered, taken in itself, quite reasonable for a fourth-grader: "A fraction is a part, it's a part of something." • What was worrying about this answer emerged when the investigator asked for examples of fractions. Almost all the examples given were of just one kind: a physical piece of a physical thing such as a slice of a pie. What is wrong with that is seen by comparing it with what the same children said four months later. After their experience as software designers, their examples became enormously varied: half an hour, twenty-five cents, a half-price sale, daytime. Debbie topped the variety of examples by her general principle, which came down to saying: "Why are you bothering me to give specific examples of fractions? . . . Don't you see that anything you think of can be an example of a fraction?"

Debbie's theory of fractions, which is quite remarkable in itself, is even more striking when contrasted with her position in the initial interview. When asked to show an example of a fraction, she drew a circle, divided it in two, shaded in the right half, and said, "There: that's a fraction; that's a half." When the investigator asked her about the unshaded side, she said, "No, that's not a fraction; that's nothing." For Debbie a "fraction" was not only a part of a physical thing, it was a shaded part of a circle. Moreover, it had to be shaded on the right side. The investigator, noticing that Debbie presented all her examples in this orientation, rotated one of her drawings so that the shaded side was up. Was that a fraction? Debbie's answer at least showed that she was thinking and not simply answering mindlessly: "Kind of," she said, "you can turn it"; and she rotated it back to the preferred position so that it now became a "fraction."

The point here is not that these restricted answers represented Debbie's total knowledge about fractions. She probably would have acquitted herself well enough in a squabble with a sibling about the distribution of candy. The point is that formal school knowledge of fractions was not connected with her intuitive everyday knowledge. What she learned in class was brittle, formal, and isolated from life. Attempts by teachers and textbook authors to connect school fractions with real life via representations as pies simply resulted in a new rigidity. Her participation in this project, on the other hand, led to more living connections. The shift in Debbie's thinking was not just a matter of knowing facts and skills. Her phrase "you can put them on top of anything" showed an epistemological shift and an epistemological intention. She made a shift from one kind of knowledge (formal, teacher's knowledge) to another kind (personal, concrete, her own). At the beginning, a "fraction" was a definite thing about which she had learned from a teacher. At the end, "fractions" meant a way of looking at the world. "Putting fractions on" something meant using them as a way of thinking about, a particular view of, whatever you put them on.

The way the shift actually happened was like this. Debbie had been trying to draw fractions on the computer screen. At first this was easy: A fraction was a divided and partly shaded circle, so she had simply to master the means needed to create such figures on the screen, as shown in the illustration on the page opposite.

An awakening new interest led her to want more varied examples, and eventually to her announcing her discovery in the designer's notebook that each of the students was asked to keep. The illustration of a page from the notebook on page 112 shows her excitement in writing it and the importance she attached to the discovery.

What made the shift happen? What led to the awakening of the new interest?

A full discussion would have to treat many aspects of a complex situation. Among these, I believe that an essential aspect was the quality of feeling "serious"—as with my newspaper and Piaget's schoolboy articles, or the assertion of national, professional, and gender pride by the Costa Rican teachers, Debbie's project moved out of the category of assignment to be gotten out of the way as soon as possible. Instead, it became a personally meaningful undertaking capable of mobilizing intellectual energy. Other interpretations are discussed in Harel's book, *Children as Software Designers*, which offers the most thorough discussion I have seen of a single experiment on children using computers.

Debbie's software design project did not have this quality of engagement from the beginning. During the first few weeks she gave it only the most desultory attention, sharing her time at the computer between somewhat listless dabbling with drawing some representations of fractions on the screen and much more energized concentration on putting up animated decorations for poems she had written about her personal feelings. One day,

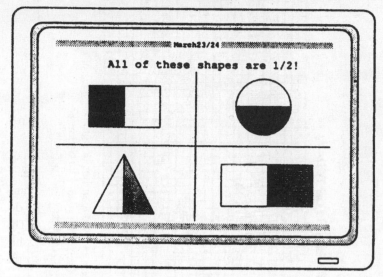

Debbie uses this screen to convey her discovery about fractions:
Fractions are everywhere.

serendipity made a connection between the two activities. She
realized that a programming technique she was using for her
decorations could be used to make her representations of a fraction more visually interesting. One thing led to another. A classmate noticed her screen and asked how she got that effect. Suddenly this girl who had led an undistinguished life as a class
member found herself in demand as an "expert" who had knowledge that others wanted. Her attitude to the software design project changed. Previously she had wanted to stay out of it as far as
she could; now, basking in her success, she wanted to be in it as
far as she could. So she started exploring, looking for fractions.

Debbie's project now started taking her "among the fractions"
in the real world around her, giving them an existence for her they
had never had before. Previously, fractions had existed only in the
classroom, and even within those narrow confines they were
further restricted to the teacher's blackboard and to Debbie's
worksheets. There was no toehold for her to explore them, to

MY PLANS FOR TODAY

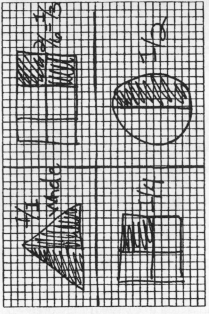

MY PLANS FOR TODAY

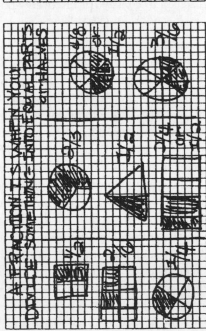

Debbie entered her plans and progress every day in her designer's notebook. Her writing at the top of the screen reads: A fraction is when you divide something into equal parts or halves.

engage with them. When she left the classroom she left them behind. No wonder she saw them nowhere except in the pie diagrams through which they were presented to her in class. Now Debbie the poet gradually began to see fractions everywhere. She was on her way to building a new relationship with fractions by allowing them into her web of real interests in defiance of School's balkanized rules: Poetry is poetry and math is math.

Kitchen Math

A recent "discovery" by ethnographers showed that women engaged in household tasks know and use more mathematics than one would suspect from Schoolish tests, only they know it in forms different from what School teaches. The cognitive anthropologist Jean Lave observed how women working in their kitchens adapted recipes to adjust the total quantity. From a Schoolish point of view this appears to be a problem in fractions (or "proportions"), but the women did not use the numerical methods they had been taught in School. Instead, they employed ad hoc "concrete" methods based on the specific situation. The results of this piece of formal research resonate with my own informal experiences (and no doubt with those of many readers).

I was momentarily shocked when a friend with whom I was cooking computed two-thirds of one-and-a-half cups of flour by the following procedure: Measure one-and-a-half cups onto the pastry board, spread it into a circle, divide the circle into three slices by making a symmetrical pie-cut pattern, and put one slice back into the flour canister. My mind "sees" one-and-a-half as three pieces (each equal to one-half) so directly that I needed time to empathize with the problem. I was helped to put this in perspective when another friend who read a draft of this text pointed out that she directly "sees" the identity of plants, whereas I go through an analytic cycle of noting leaf forms and flower structures. Still, even though she had read my account and made an intelligent comment, she had not "seen" what I "saw," since she went on to offer another solution to the flour problem that took my mathematician's breath away both for what she "saw" and for what she did not "see." She said, hesitating and presumably thinking as she went along, but with a strong voice that expressed confidence: "I would use the one-third-cup measure . . . every kitchen has one . . . you can use it twice to get two-thirds of a cup . . . and then . . . well . . . if you use it once you'll get two-thirds of half a cup . . . so that gives you two-thirds of a cup and two-thirds of half a cup." Her thought process is illustrated on the page opposite.

In my mathematician's language I redescribed this to myself as a deduction: two-thirds of half a cup equals half of two-thirds of a cup, equals one-third of a cup. But when I asked my friend to explain why her plan would work, she found no such words. The math reticence inherited from School many years before reasserted itself and she started off with: "Oh . . . One-and-a-half . . . that's five-thirds . . . isn't it?" and faded away into a little voice. The shift in voice spoke volumes. The strong voice and the competent kitchen math said she was in her territory; the little fading voice and the incompetent excursion into School math said she was in a territory which was "the other person's," as well as being especially alienating for her.

Two aspects of this, epistemological and mathetic, are important, and of course the relationship between them. Kitchen math highlights the futility of School math from a point of view that goes beyond the critique of School's ways of trying to convey knowledge. What is called in question here is the knowledge itself: Not only does School use faulty methods of teaching, what it teaches is not what people use when they have to deal with a real problem. None of us, including myself, used the abstract, formal school-math approach which would be to convert $1\frac{1}{2}$ to $\frac{3}{2}$, then do something like:

$$\frac{2}{3} * \frac{3}{2} = \frac{6}{6} = 1$$

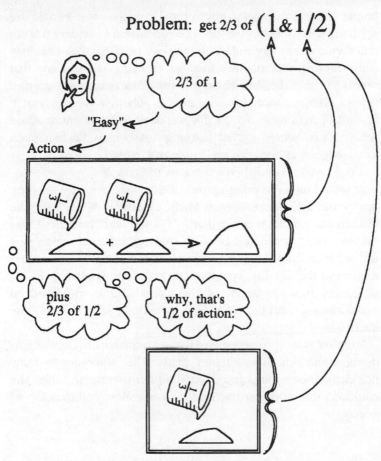

A representation of what might have been going on in the head of someone doing kitchen math.

The central epistemological moral is that we all used concrete forms of reasoning. The central mathetic moral is that in doing this we demonstrated we had learned to do something mathematical without instruction—and even despite having been taught to proceed differently.

This widespread use of mathematical methods that were not

taught is not grounds for educational complacency. People are still limited in what they can do. The conclusion to be drawn is not that they do it anyway and so do not need help, but that what they learn informally points to a form of knowing and learning that seems to come naturally to people but goes against the grain of School. The question for educators is whether we can join it instead of fighting it. To do this we need to know more about what "it" is. What kind of learning lies behind kitchen math knowledge, and how can we foster and extend it?

Could we make kitchen math part of School?

It would miss the point entirely if this were done by dressing up the old School exercises in kitchen clothing. What made the kitchen math work was not that it "felt relevant" because it was "about flour." It worked because the mathematical action was not separate from the rest of the work of baking. It was an extension of the familiar, syntonic actions of manipulating the instruments and substances of the kitchen. One could indeed make kitchen math part of School by making School part of the kitchen.

Another way is to recognize the ways in which Debbie was doing something like kitchen math. The computer became her kitchen for writing and decorating her poems, and then she could do the work on fractions as a seamless continuation of poetry.

Maria Builds a House

Debbie's story, and the one about the flour, revolve around people's sense of connection and disconnection with mathematics. In contemporary society another, ultimately more noxious, issue of disconnection dominates most people's relationship with technology. The chapter on teachers mentioned examples of the relationship being improved. The adoption of the computer as an extension of a personal style of teaching allowed something like the seamless continuation of the kitchen math. My next story allows a child to use a familiar toy as her kitchen.

"Will we really play with that? Here in school?" a fourth-grader exclaimed gleefully as he came into a room in which there was more Lego material than he had ever seen in one place. Francisco's initial surprise at meeting this kind of stuff in school was soon to be exceeded by greater surprises at how it was different from what he had at home. In addition to the familiar plastic building bricks, there were gears and motors whose uses he understood immediately, there were some more mysterious objects called "sensors," and, most remarkably, a way to connect the motors and sensors to a computer. He was told that with sensors he would make Lego models that could see and feel. He didn't quite believe that but was sure that he was going to have a great time.

Maria*, Francisco's classmate, had a more complex reaction. The pleasure of anticipating that whatever was going to happen would at least be a change from the usual class scheduled for this period was tinged with some apprehension. Sure enough, her initial feeling that this was boys' stuff was soon reinforced as the teacher, who didn't appear quite comfortable with it herself, showed a truck built by another class. The truck could be started and stopped or reversed by typing at a computer. The teacher talked most excitedly about how the truck would go into reverse by itself if it hit an obstacle. "You will soon all be able to build something like that and then you will understand how a lot of things work." Maria felt a familiar tightening in her stomach. Although she would have liked to understand how a lot of things worked, she really couldn't see herself building trucks with any enthusiasm. When she heard that the class would do this for two double periods twice a week for six weeks, her conflict turned to panic.

---

*Maria is an interpretive composite of several students. However, I am firmly convinced that any one of them could have acted and thought as I present her.

By the next week the Marias and Franciscos in the class were coping with what they learned to call the Lego-Logo workshop by creating a fourth-grade version of the "two cultures" image made famous by C. P. Snow. Francisco had picked up the idea of building a truck and went on to invent an automatic shift mechanism to put his vehicle into low gear when it had to climb a steep slope. Others like him had left the idea of a truck to build robots, fantastic "animals," and other constructions that moved, shook, spun, and made a lot of noise.

On the other side of the cultural divide Maria and three of her friends were doing something quite different. Greatly relieved to find that they were not forced to make trucks, they were building a house. They were not trying to invent a machine that would "do something." They were making something that felt familiar and was going to "be beautiful."

In this they continued what they had done with Lego when they had played with it at home as preschoolers, before their growing sophistication outpaced their limited supply of materials. Here the greater supply of Lego parts gave them a chance to do what they had previously enjoyed, but on a bigger, better, and more beautiful scale. Apart from sheer quantity of material, they did not take advantage of any special features of this Lego setup; they made no use of motors, sensors, or connections to the computer. The cultural division was dramatic and quite familiar. Technology versus art, science versus the humanities. Those of us who were aware of these issues watched, intrigued. How would these children handle the problem that C. P. Snow had found insuperable? Would they accept the divide? Could they bridge it? Would they want to do so?

It took time, but in the end Maria and her friends found their own way to cross the culture gap. Their manner of doing so is rich with insights into how the divide is rooted in our cultures and our schools, how it is linked with other divisions of style, gender, and ethnic ways, and how it can be crossed.

During the first week Maria's group learned how to exploit

the divide. Each child brought to the group's pool a ration of Lego parts. Since trade with other groups was permitted for greater flexibility in individual projects, a bartering market developed in which the parts that were most aggressively sought were precisely the motors and sensors that Maria's group did not value, while the parts that were least valued by the aggressive traders were the pretty pieces most suitable for building houses. Maria was enjoying herself in many ways. Exploiting the market to get the materials for a large and magnificent house gave her a certain entrepreneurial pleasure; solving geometric and technical problems of construction gave her a source of intellectual pleasure, and the form being taken by the product of all the work, the house, gave her aesthetic pleasure. She had found a niche. Would she settle into it and stay there?

No! By the second week there were signs of yearnings in other directions. A desire to enter the world of technology was showing itself in the way the girls looked at classmates' projects. By the third week observers saw the desire in a more concrete form when they noticed that a tiny light was blinking on and off in the deep recesses of the house. It was as if these girls wanted to take hold of the technology, but had to do so with great discretion to get past internal censors. The idea of doing anything technological went directly against the grain of their sense of identity as girls in very traditional families. They wanted to take hold of the technology, presumably they had always wanted to take hold of the technological side of the world, but had to do it, as it were, behind their own backs, almost invisible to themselves as well as to others.

Although the boys with their noisy trucks might not have considered a blinking light much of a project, the house builders were proud of their achievement, which was, in fact, less modest in its realization than in its appearance, since it brought them face to face with the computer. The story of the skirmishes they won in this encounter with the ways of computers is worth following in some detail.

The story opens with an easy step. To begin with, they had to connect the light to the interface box, which was not really different from plugging a lamp at home into an electrical outlet. The next step brought immediate gratification: Making the light go on and off by typing the words ON and OFF at the computer felt very different from turning a switch! By now the excitement was great, and this was fortunate because it gave the group a taste of success that carried them through the difficulties they would meet.

These began with the natural proposal to make the lights blink on and off automatically. The instrument available for this was the Logo language, the elements of which the girls barely knew from work with graphics that had started a few weeks before. One of them knew enough to type:

REPEAT [ON OFF]

The computer replied with an "error message," indicating that it was necessary to say how many times. They changed the instruction to:

REPEAT 10 [ON OFF]

This time the computer did not complain; the instruction was in grammatical Logo and the computer carried it out, but in a way that would be a lesson on how to interpret the adage that computers do exactly what they are told to do, neither more nor less. This is true enough in one sense. Computers do indeed do what they are told to do. But what they are told to do is not always what one thinks one is telling them to do. Nor is what they do always what it seems to be.

In this case, the computer did not seem to have done what it was told. The light came on and went off, leaving the eager observers waiting expectantly for the second blink, which never came. What was happening? The girls, surprised and frustrated, responded in a way analogous to a common habit of talking louder to people in a foreign country who don't understand a request in English: They made the command more insistent by increasing the number of blinks they thought they were telling the computer to make:

REPEAT 1000 [ON OFF]

The change didn't solve the problem, but it had an effect that gave them something to think about. The light still came on only once but stayed on for a longer time before going off. "It doesn't know the difference between lots of times and a long time," said one of the girls. "Yeah!" "It's stupid." They all laughed, but pleasure in their theory of the computer's behavior was soon replaced by frustration; it felt good to blame the machine and to have a sense of understanding its perverse behavior, but the lights were still not blinking. However, the theory did lead to constructive actions. The first action was to try to confirm the theory by trying REPEAT 10000. Yes, indeed, the light stayed on longer, as far as they could judge ten times as long, but still performed just one on-off cycle. Suggesting an experiment is a good quality for a theory; and on this occasion the experiment worked, seeming to confirm the theory. But the goal of making the lights blink had not been achieved.

Interestingly, what brought the goal closer was another, even better, quality of a theory: giving rise to insight by suggesting fruitful questions. Someone believed the theory sufficiently to ask, "But how can that happen? How can lots of times get confused with a long time?" The stupidity of machines amused the girls as a first answer, but its attractiveness as an explanatory principle soon wore thin. "I know," one of the girls said, "it goes so fast you can't see it. Computers go very fast. It really is doing it ten thousand times but they all run together." Aha! The insight proved its quality by leading to amusement and to action that would solve the problem. Maria said: "Yes, it's going too fast; tell it to slow down." After some chuckling at the idea that ten thousand blinks could happen so fast as to be invisible, someone asked, "How?" and another came in with, "Wait a sec . . . Hey, that's it! I remember you can say WAIT in Logo." So they typed:

REPEAT 10000 [ON WAIT OFF WAIT]

This was on track, but in solving a big problem it created a little one. Once more a complaint came from the computer: Just as the girls had previously failed to be specific about how many times to repeat, they now omitted to say how long to wait. So, knowing a little about Logo's ways, they tried "giving WAIT a number":

REPEAT 10000 [ON WAIT 5 OFF WAIT 5]

They had lucked out. The number was suitable and produced a blinking effect, which gave them another, this time even greater, sense of success. They still weren't quite satisfied with the way their flashing system worked but were too elated to fiddle with it that day.

The next day they played with the numbers to get a more pleasing rhythm of blinking. They settled on:

REPEAT 10000 [ON WAIT 4 OFF WAIT 10]

Making a single light blink indefinitely in the depths of a Lego house was a small step into the world of technology, but it had broken the ice. After one more session there were many blinking lights in the house. A week later the girls were using all their charm to regain possession of a motor they had traded for prettier Lego pieces: They now wanted a rotating Christmas tree in the living room. This was no mean task. Getting the gearing right for this brought them into other kinds of difficulty, this time in the realm of mechanical engineering rather than computer programming, but before their time with Lego had ended they had crossed this technical barrier as well and had built themselves in addition to a work of art and technology a first, albeit shaky, bridge across the cultural barrier.

It is a useful metaphor to think of Maria as crossing a single barrier, one that separates her from all those activities that have been programmed into her sense of identity under the labels "I can't do that" and "that's not for me." Every time she crosses the line, she comes closer to understanding that these labels are not immutable. Knowing that one can exercise choice in shaping and reshaping one's intellectual identity may be the most empowering idea one can ever achieve. For me the story of Maria has become emblematic of something more than this idea in its elemental form. It carries messages about how to exercise the choice. Maria might have decided at the outset to bite the bullet and build a truck like the boys. It is more than likely that doing so would have led to a distasteful experience and reinforced her deeper sense of what isn't for her. Instead she followed her good instincts, engaging in activities that felt right for her, while keeping herself open to an evolution in a new direction. The problem for educators is how to enhance and extend all aspects of what we see in the story. Designing Lego-Logo was a small but instructive step toward knowing how to provide material that will serve well as a technological infrastructure for suitable learning environments. But the more important side of the problem is nurturing the right kind of culture of learning.

Some educators might think that the process could have been made more efficient, and more comfortable, if a teacher had suggested the blinking light project at the outset. There are even researchers who dream of programming a computer to "diagnose" individual difficulties in such situations and prescribe paths to learning. I fear that this line of thinking risks missing an essential fact: What was empowering for Maria and her friends was not making the lights blink but finding their own way to get around their own internalized obstacles. Although a teacher might, of course, have given some guidance in this, it is hard to imagine a more delicate teaching task or one that I would be less inclined to entrust to any contemporary computer's power to make decisions. As a teacher I would see my best contribution as reviewing the story afterward in a way that would consolidate the students' awareness of how well they had done.

For example, I would want to be sure they recognized that building the house was an excellent strategy for mobilizing their own strengths and their own self-confidence in a difficult situation. The topics under discussion would not be Lego and lights and motors but ways of dealing with intellectually difficult or uncomfortable situations. They might include talk about strategies for solving problems and managing projects. And if I felt emotionally safe enough with the students, I would talk about the gender and ethnic issues. The extent to which I would politicize the discussion would depend on the context, but if the students took the initiative I would certainly talk about the political content of what they had done, not only because I think that the political dimension should not be hidden but also because without it the girls would not fully appreciate the intellectual power of their own work. The educational virtue of the Lego-Logo workshop was providing elbow room for these students to take what they found there in their own personal way. One factor that made this possible was a teaching attitude one could call demanding permissiveness: Children were expected to work hard on a project related to the themes of the workshop but were given very wide latitude in choosing the project. If permissiveness were the only factor, the same teaching attitude could solve all educational problems. It wasn't. Another kind of factor is inherent in the Lego-Logo material and in the learning culture that it supports. Many teachers strive to bring into their traditional classes something very like the teaching attitude of this workshop. But the permissiveness is deceptive, even if the intentions are good, when the demand is for children to fit into the straitjacket of the traditional curriculum, especially in subjects like math and science where the elbow room for personal appropriation is so narrow.

Funny Learning

Debbie connects with fractions and Maria with engineering. Each story has a main plot with a clearly stated happy ending. But a fine texture of smaller connections is just as important. Maria finds it funny that a thousand events can happen in a split second; one thousand may be a big number but it can be a tiny piece of time. The concept is important in itself. Much more important is the fact that she appropriated it through a joke connecting mathematics with humor, something for which there is little scope in school math.

A friend's conversation with his young daughter illustrates how a mix of the serious and the humorous happens spontaneously in certain family cultures. This favors mathematical development by slowly building a rich web of connections.

CHILD: Daddy, do you know that two is half of four?
FATHER: That's interesting. Yes, I do know. Do you know what is half of six?
CHILD (thinks for a while): Three.
FATHER: And what is half of three?
CHILD (thinks for an even longer time): Which half?
FATHER (who has to do the thinking this time to catch on): The big half.
CHILD: Two.
FATHER: And what about the other half?
CHILD (with an air of who-do-you-take-me-for): One, of course.

One would miss the point of the story without knowing the atmosphere of this family, where such things are both taken very seriously and treated with humor. "Which half?" could become a joke in the family culture, and through many such little incidents numbers would be woven into the family culture as something to play with, to joke about. What is interesting here is not that a child learned the Important Concept that even numbers have exact halves and odd numbers don't. What is interesting is that a family provides numerous little opportunities to appropriate mathematics as a warm and cozy dimension of life connected to other dimensions with which they feel comfortable.

Many humorous happenings in Logo classes share some of the quality of the family incident. An example will widen the view of how Logo computer environments can be rich in connecting incidents.

A kindergarten child, Dawn, was playing with a Logo program that allowed objects on the screen to be designed and set in motion. The interweaving paths made kinetic patterns like (though, of course, simpler than) those that had fascinated Brian and Henry. The speed of an object was controlled by typing a number. So the child could see that speed ten was much faster than speed two, and even begin to grope toward the idea that speed two is twice as fast as speed one.

After a while, Dawn became very excited and called the teacher and a friend to see something on her screen. She typed something with one finger hidden beyond the other hand so as to hide what she was typing. Everyone looked expectantly. Dawn said, "Look!" Nothing happened. Dawn said "Look, look!" and it took time for the teacher to get the point: Nothing was happening because she had set speed 0. Slowly it became clear that zero was a speed, so that standing still is moving—moving at speed zero.

I understand what happened to Dawn as a replay of an historically important mathematical event. I remember hearing when I was in the fourth or fifth grade that Hindu mathematicians discovered zero and wondering what that meant. What did they discover? Was it using a circular symbol? What they—and Dawn—discovered was that zero could be treated as a number. I have since found out that Dawn was not the only child to have made this discovery. Nor was a computer needed. Indeed, a poll of participants at a meeting of teachers showed that perhaps as many as one in ten of those who had children of their own had noticed a moment of excited joking of the form, "Are there any snakes in this house? Yes there are, there are *zero snakes.*"

The fact that many children make a similar discovery without the computer increases rather than diminishes my enthusiasm for the episode with Dawn. It shows that this is not a strange oddity about computers; it is part of the development of mathematical thinking. The computer probably contributes to making the discovery more likely and certainly to making it richer. Dawn could do more than laugh at the joke and tease the teacher and her friend: Accepting zero as a number and accepting standing still as moving with zero speed increased her scope for action. A little later she would be able to write programs in which a movement would be stopped by the command SETSPEED 0. Even more interesting, the joke can be extended. The turtle will obey the command FORWARD − 50 by going backward fifty steps. Similarly, the command to go back a negative amount will make the turtle go forward. So, negative numbers are numbers too, and their reality grows in the course of playing with the turtle.

Looking at the fine texture of Maria's experience shows other, different kinds of opportunity for incidental learning. One of these is handling experiments. The girls replay a situation that occurs over and over again in science. First they are puzzled—and this in itself makes the situation far more real than the usual school lab science experiment, which typically studies a question that has bothered nobody for the past hundred years. They discuss hypotheses and eventually decide on one that seems likely. They mount an experiment to test their hypothesis. The hypothesis is confirmed in essence but requires some modification. Sharpening the hypothesis leads to new developments that the girls pursue. This is very much like "science." It is very much not like "School science."

My stories about Debbie and Maria have a "remedial" aspect: Their protagonists are presented as improving an initially poor relationship with an area of knowledge. Being remedial is not really of the essence in the stories, for one could read them as showing how an initial healthy relationship could grow. Nevertheless, they show early stages of a healthy relationship with mathematics or technology. The next story gives an image of a much more developed relationship.

Ricky's Invention

Ricky was a fourth-grade student when he first came into the Lego lab at MIT. I don't know what he did in his first sessions. I became aware of his work when he had begun a project to make a robot that would move by vibration.

The key idea came from an observation that most people have made at some time: When machines vibrate, they tend to move. A washing machine that has gotten out of balance, besides making a lot of noise and seemingly trying to tear itself to pieces, also tends to move about unless firmly anchored. This phenomenon, sometimes called "traveling," is usually regarded as a nuisance to be overcome either by reducing the vibration of the device, or by anchoring it more securely. Ricky took a different tack. He looked at a vibrating Lego construction and thought of using the tendency to travel as a means of locomotion. This was a clear case of serendipity—turning the chance observation to advantage. It is often observed that important discoveries begin with chance observations and are attributed to "luck." But even if success in science and elsewhere is 90 percent luck, the luck does not pay off without some other ingredients: curiosity to understand and pursue it, energy, persistence, exercise of intelligence, and above all the sense of a supportive environment. Ricky shows all of them in striking fashion.

Having observed that a Lego motor travels when it vibrates, his first question was how to increase the vibration. How can it be made to vibrate more effectively?

A good principle of which Ricky showed himself to be a master in many other situations where I was able to observe him at work is to look for familiar situations where what you seek is well represented. Ricky found one by swinging his arm violently around. The movement of the arm caused his body to move in a seemingly random fashion. If this happened faster it would be "vibration." So he set out to provide the Lego motor with an arm.

This obliged Ricky to consider the question: What is an arm? The human arm is a complex system. Ricky simplified it. For his purpose, what was relevant was that the upper arm could turn about a shoulder and swing the lower arm in an uncontrolled way. So he looked around for Lego pieces that would simulate these features of the arm. It worked. The Lego motor equipped with this arm vibrated more and moved more.

The next step was to build a vehicle that would use this source of locomotion. Ricky's idea was to make a platform with legs, mount the motor on the platform, and let it vibrate. This construction turned out to have a fatal bug. When the motor was turned on it vibrated so forcefully that the entire contraption flew apart— Lego pieces flew off in all directions.

What could be done? Ricky considered two courses of action: Reduce the vibration or increase the resistance of the structure. Obviously, the second course seemed more attractive. But how was it to be executed?

The first idea was to add many braces and generally strengthen the whole thing, but it soon became apparent that this would make it so heavy that it was unlikely to move. Then came the next brilliant idea: Make it small and compact.

The motor still vibrated. The device did not fly apart. It even moved a little, but fell over as if it were tripping on its own feet. Stop the motor. Stand it up. Try again. Same result. Now what?

The solution came from a classmate. Give it feet! Why? How? Debate quickly gave way to action. It was given feet by using Lego wheels as shoes, as shown in the sketch. There was a momentary doubt about whether it was cheating to use wheels, since this was to be a wheelless vehicle. But it was quickly resolved: These

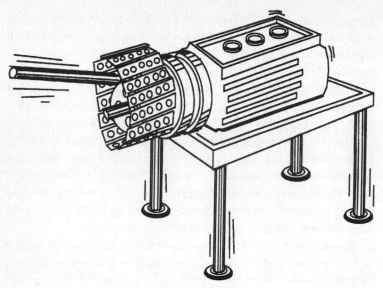

The vibrating walker.

wheels were not being used as wheels. If they had been square they would have served the purpose just as well, but round wheels were what lay at hand so they were used. Once the idea was accepted it was enjoyed with gusto, and the fact that these were wheels that were not wheels became a prominent part of Ricky's description of his work, which he was delighted to give to anyone who asked.

It worked! It worked even better than could possibly have been expected. The little machine not only moved about briskly but made an attractive, serious-sounding machine noise as it did so.

What next? You can't retire from a good project simply because it has succeeded. Playing with the robot led to a new problem and the nucleus of a solution. With its motor running, the gadget moved well enough, but it moved in a random path. Could it be steered? Again the moment of discovery was lost in the excitement, but suddenly everyone standing around it knew that when it was started it changed direction slightly. Physicists have a name for the cause of the jump: They call it conservation of angular momentum. In practice, what this means is that when the motor starts turning one way, something connected with it has to turn the other way. This may seem unbelievable—which I hope is the case (except for those who have studied physics or dance) because the statement goes against so many common observations. But Ricky and his friends did not stop to worry about what physicists might say. They had the kernel of an idea. Maybe one could steer the robot by turning the motor on and off.

Doing so required some skill but was nonetheless a solution. The machine could be steered!

Next problem: Could it steer itself to go in a more or less straight line? Yes it could, and Ricky knew pretty well how to do this. I am sure that if he had had access then to the somewhat improved technology we have today, he would have carried out the self-steering project. As it happened, doing so with the means at his disposal was too messy and needed too much help, so he preferred to turn his interest in other directions.

Although Ricky was working at a more advanced level, his method had a great deal in common with what we saw in the other stories. Like Debbie and Maria and like the practitioners of kitchen math, he worked by feeling his way. He did not follow an exact plan, although he did have a goal and was committed to realizing it; his goal was allowed to evolve as he worked. He did not build a robot by drawing on methods or materials made for that purpose; he used what he found at hand, even taking pleasure in using something made for an altogether different purpose.

Ricky's manner of working, with its elements of improvisation and of negotiating with the work in progress, is a prime example of what Sherry Turkle and I have called *bricolage*, adapting from anthropologist Claude Lévi-Strauss the use of a French word whose nearest (but inadequate) translation might be "tinkering."

Dirty Dancing

In this book I have used stories of many different kinds to build up visions of learning. Some are utterly fanciful parables, some are descriptions of actual events, some are imaginary scenarios. The next story is drawn from a movie—a fictional feature film that was not, as far as I know, made by professional specialists on learning. Stuffy academics already impatient with my unorthodox methodology might consider that this is really going too far. How can a movie be a valid source of ideas about Education?

I want here to do more than justify my use of a movie; I want to encourage everyone interested in learning to look to the general culture as a source of ideas and a basis for discussion, in the same spirit as I want to encourage looking to personal experiences. This recommendation flows from looking at learning as a dimension of life, like relationships, spirituality, or aesthetic sensibility. In all such dimensions we develop sophistication and sensitivity from works of the imagination—novels, theater, painting. These works might be "made up" in one sense, but in another they convey truths as deep as and often more accurate than experiments conducted by scientists to illuminate such topics. I believe we can learn about learning in a similar way, and would do so to a greater extent if we practiced critical discussion of this aspect of art.

There is also another reason why specialists on learning should look seriously at the representation of learning in fiction. For even if they choose to look down their noses at fiction as a source of knowledge, they can be sure that others will, possibly unconsciously, be influenced by the images of learning prevalent in the popular culture. And if these others are students, or people such as parents who influence students, their images of learning will surely affect how learning actually happens.

The movie *Dirty Dancing* is a learning story in the same sense that *Romeo and Juliet* is a love story. In its opening scenes we see

Jennifer Grey in the role of Baby, an idealistic student whose ungainly walk and posture carry the message that she was occupied with cerebral concerns when her peers were developing their sense of body and movement in physical activities. Baby is no dancer, and knows so little about dancing that she seems not to have any idea of the magnitude of the learning that will be required when she volunteers to substitute for the female partner in a spectacular dance act less than a week away. In fact, a critical teacher might attribute the same ignorance to the author of a story that shows Baby performing the act competently after a week of intensive work with the male partner (played by Patrick Swayze). For my part, I don't know whether this timing is credible, but I do know that it is much more likely to be achieved through a learning process like the one shown in the movie than through the kind of process practiced in School.

Be that as it may, the connoisseur of learning will find more of interest in the quality of Baby's experience than in speculation about the time required to achieve her goal: What made the movie compelling for me was the credibility of the features of good learning it brings into the spotlight. The fact that some of these features (among them possibly the speed of learning) are presented in a heightened, larger-than-life form appears to me as a benefit (certainly not a fault) from the use of the artistic medium, just as the high drama of the action in *Romeo and Juliet* makes it more, not less, relevant to the human issues we meet in the lower drama of our own lives.

The movie's action takes place in a resort in the Catskill Mountains, where one sees two classes of people, two kinds of dancing, and two kinds of learning. The staid, well-heeled guests are pampered in the hope that they will come back next year. The resort workers are disciplined and bullied by the threat that they might not. Although the resort is structured to keep the two classes as far apart as possible, such lines of segregation are seldom absolute, and in this case the action of the movie is precipitated by two crossings. Baby, brought by her parents to this place that has no attraction for her, restlessly wanders through its grounds and stumbles on the staff quarters where she runs into a society shockingly different from anything she has encountered in her previously sheltered existence. In it she encounters a victim of the other crossing: The dancer for whom she will later stand in is pregnant and has been abandoned by the baby's father, the owner's nephew; Baby's offer will allow her to leave the resort and have an abortion.

Baby's first shock comes from the dirty dancing. In the resort ballroom the guests dance sedately with their feet. Some shuffle formlessly in time with the music. Others follow formulaic sequences of steps: "Forward . . . forward . . . side . . . together" and "slow . . . slow . . . quick . . . quick . . . slow." In the staff quarters people dance, well, dirty. They make movements explicitly suggestive of sexual acts and touch one another erotically. But in my view the inspired phrase *dirty dancing* goes deeper than this. What is truly powerful, and deeply erotic, about the dancing is not the suggestive reference to mechanical acts of sex but the full engagement of body, of energy, of passion.

The deeper sense of what is clean and what is dirty becomes clearer if we shift the focus from dancing to learning how to dance. When dancing is defined by formula it lends itself to a familiar kind of teaching, which I propose to call "clean teaching." I think that anyone who has been to a genteel school of ballroom dancing knows what this is like. The information to be conveyed is cleanly defined. The step for the fox-trot box is forward brush side together, back brush side together. Get it? Practice a little then we'll do the forward promenade. When you get both of them we'll practice putting them together.

The relationship between learner and teacher is "clean" in that it is confined, on pain of dismissal for the teacher, to impersonal technical work on mastering a collection of steps. Finally, and most subtly, the relationship between the learner and what is learned is like a clean surgical operation: New knowledge is taken in with minimal disturbance of what is already there, and certainly with minimal impact on the learner's sense of self and of society.

We see something very different when Baby begins to work with the dance instructor. Although the movie does not make this explicit, it is safe to assume that her previous experience of dance lessons, indeed of lessons in general, would lead her to expect that the work would follow the pattern of clean learning. In fact she gets something very different. Learning "steps" is the least part of it, though there is some of that as well. Her tutor tells her to "listen to the music like a heart," and uses their slowly developing erotic relationship to draw her into a different sense of space and of her body. He has her walk dangerously across a high and narrow log bridge to develop a sense of equilibrium, posture, and confidence. What is happening to her as she learns to dance is not confined to a cleanly delimited set of emotionally neutral skills. It certainly could not be described as a "program" in any ordinary sense of that word. It includes entering a new relationship with herself. It includes changing her relationship with authority, with her father, and with the upper-crust world in which her family lives.

It is reasonable to ask whether the contrasting models of learning that I have called "clean" and "dirty" in the domain of learning to dance apply to other domains that are considered more abstract and intellectual. To feel out a response I shall probe the extent to which a parallel can be made with other more Schoolish areas, starting with the most abstract, namely, mathematics.

In some respects, on the clean side, the parallel works easily. Clean learning reduces dance to formulas describing steps, and clean learning reduces math to formulas describing procedures to manipulate symbols. The formula for a fox-trot box step is strictly analogous to the formula for adding fractions or solving equations. The other components of cleanness in dance lessons also apply directly to school math. Emotions are kept out. The relationship between teacher and student is confined to the exchange of information about the topic being studied. Certainly nothing verging on the erotic is considered to have any role.

On the side of dirty learning, the parallel might seem less clear. In representing Baby's learning as "dirty," I referred to bodily involvement, to overcoming fear, and to issues of social class. It might seem that these issues are intrinsically associated with dance but are not really part of what mathematics is about. I do agree that it seems so if one accepts the prevailing models of school math. But then it would also seem that dance is not related to such matters if one stays with the models of dance and dance learning that prevail in the guest's ballroom or in Arthur Murray's presentation of education in ballroom dancing. It is necessary to do a little deconstruction to distinguish between aspects of mathematics that have been built into the School construction of what the subject is about and those that have a stronger claim.

If one accepts what Brian and Henry were doing as math, the distance between math and dance is at least a little reduced, for they were doing something of both at the same time. They certainly were bringing more of themselves into the picture than is envisaged in the clean math class. Maria was challenging a social affiliation. Debbie was changing her sense of herself, as indeed Brian and Henry were. What I think is quite clear is that in these situations we see children moving toward the position marked out by Baby's learning. If they don't go as far, it is not because school subjects are intrinsically different from dance but because Baby was in a situation to live her relationship with dance more fully than one could hope to see in today's schools.

7

• • •

Instructionism versus Constructionism

I have tried to stay for as long as I could with a style one could loosely describe as concrete. The time has come to switch, although only for the space of one chapter, to a slightly more academic and abstract style so as to allow comparisons and interchange with other points of view. In doing so I shall also work at sharpening and formalizing (which does not necessarily mean improving) mathetic ideas that I have introduced up to now mainly by way of stories.

My preference for a concrete way of writing is not simply a literary tactic for saying what I could have expressed in more abstract language. Rather, it is a case of making the medium the message. A central theme of my message is that a prevailing tendency to overvalue abstract reasoning is a major obstacle to progress in education. One of several possible formulations of my view of how learning might become very different is that this will come about through an epistemological reversion to more concrete ways of knowing—a reversal of the traditional idea that intellectual progress consists of moving from the concrete to the abstract. Moreover, I see the need for the reversal not only in the content of what is learned but also in the discourse of the educators. Using a concrete mode of expression myself allows me to show as well as say what I mean by this, and contributes to a richer sense of what makes concrete thinking powerful. However, it is not surprising that the concept most in need of a more abstract formulation is "concreteness" itself.

In the discourse of education, the word *concrete* is often used in its everyday sense. When teachers talk about using concrete materials to support learning the idea of numbers, one easily understands that this embraces such methods as using wooden blocks to form number patterns. But the word has also acquired more specialized meanings, of which the most prominent is closely associated with Jean Piaget's famous (or, in some circles, infamous) theory of stages. Unfortunately the two kinds of use are often confounded: It is easy to fall into the trap of reading Piaget as if the word had its ordinary meaning, and the fallacy is supported by the many books written in a patronizing tone on the lines of "Piaget made easy" for teachers. In fact, Piaget is doing something more complex and much more interesting when he describes the thinking of children of elementary school age as "concrete." This is as much a technical term as the physicists' use of the word *force* or psychiatrists' use of the word *depression*—in all these cases meanings will be misunderstood unless one realizes that the words get a special twist from theories that often go against the grain of common sense. Piaget's concept of "concrete intelligence" gets its meaning from a theoretical perspective that emerged slowly, and not always consistently, in the course of an enormously productive lifelong enterprise of research. We shall have to disentangle this very insightful concept from certain more problematic aspects of Piaget's theoretical constructions, in particular his notion of "stage." The opposition of educational philosophies that forms the title of the chapter provides a good context for pinning down what "concrete intelligence" means in Piaget's theoretical framework.

The suffix -*ism* is a marker of the abstract and its presence in the title reflects my shift in intellectual style. The word *instructionism* is intended to mean something rather different from *pedagogy,* or the art of teaching. It is to be read on a more ideological or programmatic level as expressing the belief that the route to better learning must be the improvement of instruction—if School is less than perfect, why then, you know what to do: Teach better. Constructionism is one of a family of educational philosophies that denies this "obvious truth." It does not call in question the value of instruction as such. That would be silly: Even the statement (endorsed if not originated by Piaget) that every act of teaching deprives the child of an opportunity for discovery is not a categorical imperative against teaching, but a paradoxically expressed reminder to keep it in check. The constructionist attitude to teaching is not at all dismissive because it is minimalist—the goal is to teach in such a way as to produce the most learning for the least teaching. Of course, this cannot be achieved simply by reducing the quantity of teaching while leaving everything else unchanged. The principal other necessary change parallels an African proverb: If a man is hungry you can give him a fish, but it is better to give him a line and teach him to catch fish himself.

Traditional education codifies what it thinks citizens need to know and sets out to feed children this "fish." Constructionism is built on the assumption that children will do best by finding ("fishing") for themselves the specific knowledge they need; organized or informal education can help most by making sure they are supported morally, psychologically, materially, and intellectually in their efforts. The kind of knowledge children most need is the knowledge that will help them get more knowledge. This is why we need to develop mathetics. Of course, in addition to knowledge about fishing, it is as well to have good fishing lines, which is why we need computers, and to know the location of rich waters, which is why we need to develop a large range of mathetically rich activities or "microworlds."

Take mathematics once more, to see the general issue in its most extreme form. It is obvious that as a society we in the United States (and most places in the world) are mathematical underachievers. It is also obvious that instruction in mathematics is on the average rather poor. But it does not follow that the only route to better performance is the improvement of instruction. Another route goes via offering children truly interesting microworlds in which they can *use* mathematics as Brian did, or *think about* it as Debbie did, or *play* with it as Dawn did. If children really want to learn something, and have the opportunity to learn it in use, they do so even if the teaching is poor. For example, many learn difficult video games with no professional teaching at all! Others use Nintendo's system of telephone hot lines or read magazines on strategies for games to find the kind of advice for video games that they would get from a teacher if this were a school subject. Moreover, since one reason for poor instruction is that nobody likes to teach reluctant children, the constructionist route will make teaching better as well as less necessary, thus achieving the best of both worlds.

Debbie provides a good example of a little of the right instruction going a long way. Instruction in programming the computer and thinking about how to develop a complex project was like teaching her to catch fish. With these skills she could build her software and transform her thinking about fractions. She learned something very different from what she was taught. This is very different from something that used to be called *process learning*. In the 1960s, at the same time as the New Math movement reached its peak, it was fashionable to say that it was more important to teach "the process of scientific thinking" than any particular scientific content. The significant difference is that scientific process divorced from content is very abstract. The programming skills Debbie learned were even more down-to-earth and concrete in every possible sense than the knowledge about fractions she acquired by using them.

Debbie's success in the test on knowledge of fractions goes against the instructionist idea that the unique way to improve a student's knowledge about topic X is to teach about X. Anyone who has doubts about the prevalence of this idea would do well to read Ivan Illich's *Deschooling Society,* again in the spirit of seeing an idea starkly through its extreme form. Illich eloquently states his case that the principal lesson School teaches is the need to be taught. School's teaching creates a dependence on School and a superstitious addiction to belief in its methods. But while School's self-serving lesson has pervaded world culture, what is most remarkable is that we all have personal experience and personal knowledge that go against it. On some level we know that if we become really involved with an area of knowledge, we learn it—with or without School, and in any case without the paraphernalia of curriculum and tests and segregation by age groups that School takes as axiomatic. We also know that if we do not become involved with the area of knowledge, we'll have trouble learning it with or without School's methods. In the context of a School-dominated society, the most important principle of mathetics may be the incitement to revolt against accepted wisdom that comes from knowing you can learn without being taught and often learn best when taught least.

Kitchen math points up the same moral; it shows that a large number of people have learned to do something mathematical without instruction—and even despite having been taught to do something else. Indeed, it may even suggest that there is no real crisis in education after all, since people with a will do find a way to learn what they need!

Of course, this complacent suggestion is not serious. Pointing to the use of mathematical methods that were somehow developed without being taught cannot justify educational complacency: Kitchen math and the like are wonderful demonstrations of people's mathetic capacity, but they are extremely limited. The conclusion to be drawn is not that people manage anyway and so do not need help, but rather that this informal learning points to a rich form of natural learning that goes against the grain of School's methods and needs a different kind of support. The question for educators is whether we can work with this natural learning process rather than against it—and to do this we need to know more about what the process is. What kind of learning lies behind kitchen math knowledge, and how can we foster and extend it?

These questions move us to the second pole of "instructionism versus constructionism." The poor reflection on School is a minor aspect of what one can see in kitchen math. The major aspect is not the failure of School but the success of the people who had developed their own methods for solving such problems—not what School failed to convey to them but what they constructed for themselves.

The metaphors of conveying and constructing are the pervasive themes of a larger and more variegated educational movement within which I situate constructionism and underscore this by the wordplay in its name. For many educators and all cognitive psychologists, my word will evoke the term *constructivism,* whose contemporary educational use is most commonly referred back to Piaget's doctrine that knowledge simply cannot be "transmitted" or "conveyed ready made" to another person. Even when you seem to be successfully transmitting information by telling it, if you could see the brain processes at work you would observe that your interlocutor is "reconstructing" a personal version of the information you think you are "conveying." *Constructionism* also has the connotation of "construction set," starting with sets in the literal sense, such as Lego, and extending to include programming languages considered as "sets" from which programs can be made, and kitchens as "sets" with which not only cakes but recipes and forms of mathematics-in-use are constructed. One of my central mathetic tenets is that the construction that takes place "in the head" often happens especially felicitously when it is supported by construction of a more public sort "in the world"—a sand castle or a cake, a Lego house or a corporation, a computer program, a poem, or a theory of the universe. Part of what I mean by "in the world" is that the product can be shown, discussed, examined, probed, and admired. It is out there.

Thus, constructionism, my personal reconstruction of constructivism, has as its main feature the fact that it looks more closely than other educational *-isms* at the idea of mental construction. It attaches special importance to the role of constructions in the world as a support for those in the head, thereby becoming less of a purely mentalist doctrine. It also takes the idea of constructing in the head more seriously by recognizing more than one kind of construction (some of them as far removed from simple building as cultivating a garden), and by asking questions about the methods and the materials used. How can one become an expert at constructing knowledge? What skills are required? And are these skills the same for different kinds of knowledge?

The name *mathetics* gives such questions the recognition needed to be taken seriously. To begin answering them I shall discuss and adapt somewhat to present purposes the ideas of two thinkers, Jean Piaget and Claude Lévi-Strauss, who went as far as anyone in identifying large pockets of knowledge that are not learned in School's way and do not conform to School's idea of what proper knowing is. My purpose in discussing both of these authors here is to derive from them a technical sense of the notion of concreteness that will allow me to say that the important mathetic skill is that of constructing concrete knowledge. Later on I use this insight for another formulation of what is wrong with School—that its perverse commitment to moving as quickly as possible from the concrete to the abstract results in spending minimal time where the most important work is to be done.

In his 1966 book *The Savage Mind* (whose French title, *La pensée sauvage,* should be read with an awareness that in French wildflowers are called *fleurs sauvages*), Lévi-Strauss adopts the untranslatable French word *bricolage* to refer to how "primitive" societies conduct "a science of the concrete." He sees this as different from the "analytic science" of his own colleagues in a way that parallels the difference between kitchen math and school math. School math, like the ideology, though not necessarily the practice, of modern science, is based on the ideal of generality— the single, universally correct method that will work for all problems and for all people. *Bricolage* is a metaphor for the ways of the old-fashioned traveling tinker, the jack-of-all-trades who knocks on the door offering to fix whatever is broken. Faced with a job, the tinker rummages in his bag of assorted tools to find one that will fit the problem at hand and, if one tool does not work for the job, simply tries another without ever being upset in the slightest by the lack of generality.

The basic tenets of *bricolage* as a methodology for intellectual activity are: Use what you've got, improvise, make do. And for the true *bricoleur* the tools in the bag will have been selected over a long time by a process determined by more than pragmatic utility. These mental tools will be as well worn and comfortable as the physical tools of the traveling tinker; they will give a sense of the familiar, of being at ease with oneself; they will be what Illich calls "convivial" and I called "syntonic" in *Mindstorms*. Here I use the concept of *bricolage* to serve as a source of ideas and models for improving the skill of making—and fixing and improving—mental constructions. I maintain that it is possible to work systematically toward becoming a better *bricoleur,* and offer this as an example of developing mathetic skill. One sees the spirit of the true *bricoleur* most directly in the story of Ricky's ingenuity (and delight) in using Lego parts for purposes that were never imagined by their makers: a wheel as a shoe, a motor as a vibrator. One also sees in this use of Lego-Logo a microworld strongly conducive to the skills of *bricolage.* And I see it in my experience with plants.

Kitchen math provides a clear demonstration of *bricolage* in its seamless connection with a surrounding ongoing activity that provides the tinker's bag of tricks and tools. The opposite of *bricolage* would be to leave the "cooking microworld" for a "math world," to work the fractions problem using a calculator or, more likely in this case, mental arithmetic. But the practitioner of kitchen math, as a good *bricoleur,* does not stop cooking and turn to math; on the contrary, the mathematical manipulations of ingredients would be indistinguishable to an outside observer from the culinary manipulations. Thus kitchen math exhibits the quality of connectedness, of continuity, that I have presented several times as so powerfully conducive to learning. This embeddedness sharply illuminates the relationship between the mathetic question of instructionism versus constructionism and the epistemological question of analytic science versus *bricolage*. Analytic principles such as multiplying 1½ by ⅔ are routinely taught through direct instruction in math. But the close association of kitchen math with the kitchen suggests that it is not natural, even if it is possible, to "teach" mathematical (or any other kind of) *bricolage* as a separate subject. The natural context for learning would be through participation in other activities than the math itself.

A comparison between Debbie and kitchen math brings out the special role of the computer in doing this. I have no doubt at all that increased skill and confidence would come to many people if they engaged in more respectful and thoughtful talk about their learning processes in cooking, gardening, home maintenance, games, and participation in sports whether as player or spectator. None of this absolutely requires computers. What we see in experiences like those of Debbie or Maria or Brian is how the computer simply, but very significantly, enlarges the range of opportunities to engage as a *bricoleur* or *bricoleuse* in activities with scientific and mathematical content.

The phases of Debbie's experience show an expanding extension of engagement and competence through a *bricoleur*ish type of appropriation. In the first phase we see her engaged in a familiar activity minimally transformed by being done on the computer. She writes poems using the computer as little more than a word processor. Then she decorates her poems much as she might decorate a paper page. It is only when she is thoroughly comfortable with doing this that she begins to do anything interesting with fractions. Then we see her engaged in activities that are concerned with fractions; but in the same way as kitchen math is not separate from cooking, these activities are not distinguishable in form from the poetry work. And it is precisely this continuation of the familiar into the new that brings her breakthrough to connecting fractions with "everything."

This praise for the concrete is not to be confused with a strategy of using it as a stepping-stone to the abstract. That would leave the abstract ensconced as the ultimate form of knowing. I want to say something more controversial and more subtle in helping to demote abstract thinking from being seen as "the real stuff" of the working of the mind. More often, if not always in the last analysis, concrete thinking is more deserving of this description, and abstract principles serve in the role of tools that serve, like many others, to enhance concrete thinking. For the confirmed *bricoleur,* formal methods are on tap, not on top. In the kitchen, formal multiplication of 1½ by ⅔ is a perfectly acceptable method, no worse, but no better, than improvisations with spatulas and measuring cups.

Statements like this have brought down on my head accusations of "logic bashing." But the issue is really one of balance. I am a mathematician and know firsthand the marvels of abstract reasoning. I know its pleasures as well as its power. I also know how stultifying it can be if it is used indiscriminately. Our intellectual culture has traditionally been so dominated by the identification of good thinking with abstract thinking that the achievement of balance requires constantly being on the lookout for ways to reevaluate the concrete, one might say, as an epistemological analog of affirmative action. It also requires being on the lookout for insidious forms of abstractness that may not be recognized as such by those who use them. For example, styles of programming that are often imposed as if they were simply "the right way" express a strong value judgment between the abstract and the concrete ways of doing things.

In her book *The Second Self,* Sherry Turkle describes styles of programming used by children who were given sufficient access to computers and a sufficient sense of freedom in developing a personal style:

Jeff is the author of one of the first space-shuttle programs. He does it, as he does most other things, by making a plan. There will be a rocket, boosters, a trip through the stars, a landing. He conceives the program globally; then he breaks it up into manageable pieces. "I wrote out the parts on a big piece of cardboard. I saw the whole thing in my mind just in one night, and I couldn't wait to come to school to make it work." Computer scientists will recognize this global "top-down," "divide-and-conquer" strategy as "good programming style." And we all recognize in Jeff someone who conforms to our stereotype of a "computer person" or an engineer—someone who would be good with machines, good at science, someone organized, who approaches the world of things with confidence and sure intent, with the determination to make it work.

Kevin is a very different sort of child. Where Jeff is precise in all of his actions, Kevin is dreamy and impressionistic. Where Jeff tends to try to impose his ideas on other children, Kevin's warmth, easygoing nature, and interest in others make him popular. Meetings with Kevin were often interrupted by his being called out to rehearse for a school play. The play was *Cinderella,* and he had been given the role of Prince Charming. . . ,

Kevin too is making a space scene. But the way he goes about it is not at all like Jeff's approach. Jeff doesn't care too much about the detail of the form of his rocket ship; what is important is getting a complex system to work together as a whole. But Kevin cares more about the aesthetics of the graphics. He spends a lot of time on the shape of his rocket. He abandons his original idea but continues to "doodle" with the scratchpad shape-maker. He works without plan, experimenting, throwing different shapes onto the screen. He frequently stands back to inspect his work, looking at it from different angles, finally settling on a red shape against a black night—a streamlined, futuristic design. He is excited and calls over two friends. One admires the red on the black. The other says that the red shape "looks like fire." Jeff happens to pass Kevin's machine on the way to lunch and automatically checks out its screen, since he is always looking for new tricks to add to his tool kit for building programs. He shrugs. "That's been done." Nothing new there, nothing technically different, just a red blob. . . .

By the next day Kevin has a rocket with red fire at the bottom. "Now I guess I should make it move . . . moving and wings . . . it should have moving and wings." The wings turn out to be easy, just some more experimenting with the scratchpad. But he is less certain about how to get the moving right. Kevin knows how to write programs, but his programs emerge, he is not concerned with imposing his will on the machine. He is concerned primarily with creating exciting visual effects and allows himself to be led by the effects he produces.

The supervaluation of the abstract blocks progress in education in mutually reinforcing ways in practice and in theory. In the practice of education the emphasis on abstract-formal knowledge is a direct impediment to learning—and since some children, for reasons related to personality, culture, gender, and politics, are harmed more than others, it is also a source of serious discrimination if not downright oppression. Kevin is lucky to be in an environment where he is allowed to work in his own style. In many schools he would be under pressure to do things "properly," and even if his way of working were tolerated, there might be a snide sense that this is because he is "artistic," said with a tone that implies he is not a serious academic student. For example, in interviews reported in a paper written jointly with me, Turkle was told by a female student that the pressure to follow Jeff's kind of "hard" style was so great and so contrary to her sense of herself that she "decided to become someone else" in order to survive a compulsory course. Others in a similar situation simply dropped out.

Furthermore, the supervaluation of abstract thinking vitiates discussion of educational issues. The reason is that educators who advocate imposing abstract ways of thinking on students almost always practice what they preach—as I tried to do in adopting a concrete style of writing—but with very different effects.

A simple example is seen in the formulation of research questions. In front of me is a stack of learned papers, filled with numbers, tables, and statistical formulas, with titles such as "An Assessment of the Effect of the Computer on Learning." Their authors would be indignant at the suggestion that their work is "abstract." They would surely say that the shoe is on the other foot: They have produced "concrete numerical data," in marked contrast with my "abstract anecdotal philosophizing." But however concrete their data, any statistical question about "the effect" of "the computer" is irretrievably abstract. This is because all such questions depend on the use of what is often called "scientific method," in the form of experiments designed to study the effect of one factor which is varied while taking great pains to keep everything else the same. The method may be perfectly appropriate for determining the effect of a drug on a disease: When researchers try to compare patients who have had the drug with those who have not, they go to great pains to be sure that nothing else is different. But nothing could be more absurd than an experiment in which computers are placed in a classroom where nothing else is changed. The entire point of all the examples I have given is that the computers serve best when they allow *everything* to change.

The point of abstract thinking is to isolate—to abstract—a pure essential factor from the details of a concrete reality. In some sciences this has been done with marvelous results. For example, Sir Isaac Newton was able to understand the motions of the earth and the moon around the sun by representing each of these complex bodies by a concretely absurd "abstraction"—by treating each body as a particle with its entire mass concentrated at one point he could apply his equations of motion. Although it has been the dream of many psychologists to possess a similar science of learning, so far nothing of the sort has been produced. I believe that this is because the idea of a "science" in this sense simply does not apply here, but even if I am wrong, while we are waiting for the Newton of education to be born, different modes of understanding are needed. Specifically, in my view we need a methodology that will allow us to stay close to concrete situations.

Not long ago this suggestion would have been seen as inconsistent with the very idea of the scientific method. However, in the past few decades anthropologists have been more diligent than Lévi-Strauss was in examining the actual behavior of scientists in their laboratories with the same rigor as he applied to examining the ways of distant villages. Bruno Latour, one of the leading figures in this movement, finds that the theoretical line between the science of the concrete and analytic science is blurry and frequently transgressed by ways of thinking and acting that are closer to what Lévi-Strauss describes as *pensée sauvage* than to "analytic science." The concept of the highly rigorous and formal scientific method that most of us have been taught in school is really an ideology proclaimed in books, taught in schools, and argued by philosophers, but widely ignored in the actual practice of science. For Latour, Lévi-Strauss's " 'grand dichotomy' with its self-righteous certainty should be replaced by many uncertain and unexpected divides."

Such observations have come from many other sources—including feminist scholars, who have argued that traditional science is strongly androcentric, and Sherry Turkle and myself, who have observed that some of the best professional programmers work in a style more like Kevin than like Jeff. These data must be taken seriously by educators, and they have multiple implications for thinking about School.

The simplest and most immediate observation, from an instructionist point of view, is the need to offer children a more modern image of the nature of science. The point here is not simply bringing the content of school science up to date, which is being done even if too slowly, but giving children a better sense of the nature of scientific activity, a goal that does not easily fit into School and is therefore almost entirely neglected. It is important to bring about these changes in science education both for the high-minded reason of respect for truth in education and, especially, for the mundane reason that the image traditionally presented repels students who would be attracted to the life of science if they only knew what it was really like, and to scientific thinking if they only knew how much it was like their own.

From a constructionist point of view there is a deeper implication, which I introduce by reopening the discussion of some important observations of children by Jean Piaget and his colleagues. Essentially, Piaget had made the same observation as Lévi-Strauss, except that where the anthropologist had looked at *la pensée sauvage* in distant societies, Piaget looked at *la pensée sauvage* close to home, in children. What they both saw was thinking that differed from "our" norms and yet had a degree of inner coherence that forbade dismissing it as simply erroneous. Both saw their findings as an important discovery of an unsuspected way of thinking; both gave what they saw a name, each using the word *concrete*—in one case as "the science of the concrete" and in the other as "the stage of concrete operations." Both set out to investigate the workings of concrete thinking paralleling the investigation of laws of abstract thought that had been studied since ancient Greek times. Both gave us valuable insights into the workings of a nonabstract way of thinking. And both had the same blind spot. They failed to recognize that the concrete thinking they had discovered was not confined to the underdeveloped—neither to Lévi-Strauss's "undeveloped" societies nor to Piaget's not yet "developed" children. Children do it, people in Pacific and African villages do it, and so do the most sophisticated people in Paris or Geneva.

Moreover, and this is what is of the most central importance, the sophisticates do not resort to "concrete thinking" only in their preliminary gropings toward solving a problem or when they are operating as novices outside their areas of expertise. As I noted in citing Latour, features of what Lévi-Strauss and Piaget identify as "concrete" are present at the core of important and sophisticated intellectual enterprises. It is hard to give examples without too wide a digression into a technical discussion of a particular science. Feminist scholars who want to make a similar point in arguing that the supervaluation of the abstract is androcentric are fond of citing Evelyn Fox Keller's biography of the Nobel Prize—winning biologist Barbara McClintock. Keller's account gives an important role to an incident that is easily citable in nontechnical language: McClintock has become as well known for saying that she studied plants by getting to know them as individuals and cells by getting inside them than for the important genetic discoveries she made. The image of McClintock shrinking into the cell has a vividness that conveys a certain sense of an anti-abstract approach, but to appreciate the point in more than a superficial way, you should read Keller's book or look for new additions to the burgeoning field of criticism of traditional epistemology.

It might be more accurate to describe the blind spot I attributed to Piaget and Lévi-Strauss as "resistance," in the sense that Freud uses when he explains reluctance to accept his theories as a manifestation of what the theory predicts—a repression of the unacceptable aggressive or sexual content of the unconscious. In Piaget's case the unacceptable is the possibility that good thinking might not conform to the standards that have been set up by generations of epistemologists. The repression consists of accepting the existence and effectiveness of such thinking but relegating it to children. Readers who have battled with Piaget's writing might even go a step further with me in speculating that Piaget is protecting himself from acknowledging that his own thinking has more of the *bricoleur* than of the formal and analytic standards of the dominant epistemology. But whatever the ultimate reason, the fact is that Piaget hid the light of his best discovery under the bushel of his theory of stages.

In outline, Piaget's theory presents intellectual development as divided into three great epochs, which (by coincidence or otherwise) approximately match three major periods in the timetable of life as seen by School. The first epoch, called the "sensorimotor stage," is roughly the same as the preschool period. This is a period of prelogic in which children respond to their immediate situation. The second epoch, which Piaget calls the stage of "concrete operations," is roughly coextensive with the elementary-school years. This is a period of concrete logic in which thought goes far beyond the immediate situation but still does not work through the operation of universal principles. Instead, its methods are still tied to specific situations, like those of an expert at kitchen math who is incapable of handling a pencil-and-paper test on fractions. And finally there is the "formal stage," which covers high school—and the rest of life. Now at last thought is driven, and disciplined, by principles of logic, by deduction, by induction, and by the principle of developing theories by the test of empirical verification and refutation.

This neat picture of successive stages has aroused such strong positive and negative reactions that the ensuing debates have obscured Piaget's really important contribution: His description of different ways of knowing is far more important than quibbling about whether they neatly follow one another chronologically. And what is especially important is the description of the nature and the development of the middle stage of concrete operations. This is the task to which he devoted the greater part of his mature life and the topic of all but a handful of the more than one hundred books he wrote about how children think in a staggering range of domains, including logic, number, space, time, motion, life, causality, machines, games, dreams.

Piaget's descriptions of thousands of conversations with children fit well with Lévi-Strauss's image of the *bricoleur*. The child will bring to bear on a situation a way of thinking about it that might be very different from what is used in a seemingly logically equivalent problem. Where Piaget has something very different to add is in his focus on change over periods of years. For example, he has conversations with children as young as four about situations involving number.

The best-known examples are the so-called conservation experiments. In one of these, children whose ages vary from four to seven are shown a row of egg cups, each containing an egg, and are asked whether there are more eggs or more egg cups. The typical response at all ages is "no" or "the same." The eggs are then removed from the egg cups and spread out in a long row while the egg cups are brought together in a tight cluster, all in full view of the child. The same question is posed. This has been done often enough, and under sufficiently varied conditions, to justify asserting with confidence that virtually all children of four or five will say "more eggs." They will defend this position under extensive cross-questioning and even when pressure is placed on them to change their minds, for example, by being told that three other children all said there were not more eggs, or by being asked to count the eggs and the egg cups. Most children will resist falling in line with the others, and one neatly commented after counting: "They count the same but it's more eggs." Thus the first remarkable observation from the experiment is that these children seem to hold a view contrary to something that is absolutely obvious to any adult—indeed, so obvious that nobody seems to have noticed before Piaget that children did not share our self-evident truth. The point is not simply that the children do not know the adult answer to the question and flounder in ignorance; the point is that they firmly and consistently give a different answer.

A sensible objection that casts light on what is really being learned is that the children are more likely to have misunderstood the question than to hold the bizarre "nonconservationist" opinion: They think they are being asked about the space occupied and not about the number. In one sense the objection must be true. If the children really understood the question as we do, they would answer as we do. But the objection deepens rather than trivializes Piaget's experiment. There may indeed be a misunderstanding, but it is not a "mere verbal misunderstanding." It reflects something deep about the child's mental world. If one suspected an adult of such misunderstanding, one would say, "No, I mean number, not space." However, saying this to a four-year-old will serve no purpose, for the child does not know how to make the distinction. Number is what you see on "Sesame Street," and space is where you sit. Neither is relevant to the distinction about eggs and egg cups. The possibility of the misunderstanding shows the state of development of this area of a child's knowledge. The work being done in the concrete period is that of gradually growing the relevant mental entities and giving them connections so that such distinctions become meaningful. When you or I see six eggs, the sixness is as much part of what we see as the whiteness or the shapes of the individual objects. As with Debbie, for us number (like fractions) is something we "put on" everything. But we must "have" it before we can do so, and it seems that for a sensorimotor child it is either not there or, like the early Debbie's fractions, too rigidly anchored to be manipulated. Following this thought, I see phenomena that Piaget ascribes to the stage of concrete operations as models for how fractions developed for Debbie or how "flowerness" and "familyness" (in the botanical sense) developed for me. In this view the educational implications of Piaget's ideas are reversed. Most of his followers in education set out to hasten (or at least consolidate) the passage of the child beyond concrete operations. My strategy is to strengthen and perpetuate the typical concrete process even at my age. Rather than pushing children to think like adults, we might do better to remember that they are great learners and to try harder to be more like them. While formal thinking may be able to do much that is beyond the scope of concrete methods, the concrete processes have their own power.

It is impossible not to feel frustrated in thinking about the nature of concrete knowledge by the advantages enjoyed by the traditional epistemology. Its unit of knowledge is a clearly demarcated entity—a proposition—and there is a well-developed, widely accepted language in which to talk about it. Part of the gap one encounters in developing any alternative epistemology is the result of time: Starting fresh, we are essentially at a disadvantage. Part of the gap is very likely to be permanent, for an epistemology predicated on pluralism and on connection between domains is bound to be less clear-cut, more complex.

A third kind of gap, which is of a more subtle nature, is the relationship of knowledge to media. The traditional epistemology is based on the proposition, so closely linked to the medium of text—written and especially printed. *Bricolage* and concrete thinking always existed but were marginalized in scholarly contexts by the privileged position of text. As we move into the computer age and new and more dynamic media emerge, this will change. Although it might be futile to outguess such radical departures in ways of dealing with knowledge, it will be interesting to keep the question in mind as we turn now to look more directly at some aspects of the history of computers in relation to epistemology and learning.

8

• • •

Computerists

THE pioneers who made the first computers knew exactly what kind of work the machines would do and what style of mind they would serve. It was the 1940s. The world was at war. Complex calculations had to be done under time pressures not normally felt by mathematicians: numerical calculations related to the design and use of weapons; logical manipulations to break ever more complex codes before the information became old news. The pioneers were mathematicians and built the machines in their own image. It is unlikely that they gave even a passing thought to making computers user-friendly to people with softer styles than theirs. The conditions were set for the development of a computer culture with no room for pluralism; its epistemological norms would be firmly planted in the most analytic tradition. It was inevitably a culture of "hards."

Wartime conditions were not the only factor shaping the computer culture in this way. The stage of development of the technology acted in the same direction. The very appearance of the early machines would strike terror into the technologically faint of heart. The first one I saw (the British ACE designed by Alan Turing himself) looked less like a machine than a robots' library with racks of electronics in place of books. No way of using it would have made it congenial to a technophobic teacher tentatively exploring her first relationship with a machine! In addition to their appearance, the technical weakness of the machines contributed to forcing a very hard-edged way of using them. Interfaces like those that make today's computers more "friendly" require lots of surplus computer power. In those days one always had to squeeze the last ounce of power from the machine to get even the simplest jobs done, and this often meant carrying out contortions of mathematical computation in one's own mind. I remember my first experiences of programming as being much more like solving problems in number theory than the self-expressive activity I ascribed to Debbie or Brian or the Costa Rican teachers. The point I am making is not simply that this was a mathematical culture (which it was), but that it was the particular kind of mathematical culture in which precise calculation plays the dominant role and the technical and analytic have more weight than the intuitive and the experiential.

Thus, many factors conspired to cast the early computer culture in the hard and analytic shape that for most people remains even today synonymous with the word *computer*. After the war the computer slowly moved out of the sanctums of high science and the military into a wider world of business and run-of-the-mill industrial and university research. As it did so it took its culture with it, and so the popular image of the computer as "analytical logic engine" grew up and took root. What is significant here is how elements of the original computer culture persisted even when the technology no longer required or favored them. Once launched, the culture acquires a logic of its own. Although some of the mathematical extremes of the early ways to control computers were gradually softened, the hard core remained.

When I programmed the ACE I actually had to express instructions as sequences of 0s and 1s coded by literally punching holes one by one in an IBM card. I do not remember the code, but similar codes still exist for modern machines: For example, the sequence 11000010111010111000001000111100 could be an instruction to the central processor to add the numbers in two given memory positions. But although these codes still have theoretical importance, someone writing a program today rarely uses them as the actual medium of expression.

Expressing instructions as binary numbers is too opaque and tedious even for a mathematician to find comfortable. It did not take long before computer languages were developed to allow an instruction to be expressed in a form more like $z = x + y$, to mean that the numbers in the memory positions x and y are added together and the result placed in memory location z. One of the intellectually powerful facts about computers is that they can manipulate their own programs: Since the computer can be programmed to translate $z = x + y$ into the appropriate binary number, the only time it is absolutely necessary to use the binary code is to write the program that does the translation.

The development of more transparent and congenial forms of expression did not mean an end to the hard-edged analytic style of thinking in programming; it only softened its most obtrusive manifestations. The mark of the mathematician was still there in the algebraic form of the instruction, and it was stamped on the culture of programming in deeper ways than this. As one might have expected, it was mathematicians with a hard-edged bent of mind who were most inclined to create theories of the proper structure of a computer program and make the effort to set up standards for the process of writing one. The result was to consolidate their view of programming as the only right one. Thus a new kind of factor became visible, which still buttresses the hard-edged computer culture today. The hards have an advantage in the ability and desire to offer theoretical justifications for their ways of doing things. A similar self-perpetuating factor works through the recruitment of people. The dominance of the hard-edged style in the culture draws new recruits who think in that way, and discourages those who would tend to push its development in another, softer direction.

As the computer spread to wider worlds of application, the idea of using it in education was bound to come up. Indeed, by the early 1960s an unfamiliar set of actors had become visible on the fringes of the education scene. The technology we brought with us (for I was one of these computerists attracted by the prospect of change in education) was extraordinarily primitive. A typical project of the time would sit a child in front of a clattering teletype machine connected with a distant computer that was too big and expensive to bring to the child. There was none of the graphics, the color, the action, and the sounds that contribute to the excitement of the computers children know and love today. Very little of what was actually done or learned under such circumstances is directly applicable today. But in contrast with the ephemerality of the technological forms of those days stands the resilience of the theoretical orientations—the ideologies—we brought with us from the larger computer culture.

The important and lasting side of what we did was planting the seed of a specifically educational computer culture. The theme of this chapter is the development of this seed into a tree with so many branches that I shall have to be selective in discussing them. In selecting the branches that seem most important I have concentrated on those in which I have been most active. I hope this is not because I see importance only where I have worked; I prefer to believe that this is because I have tried to work in the areas that are most important.

The easiest way to tell the history of the educational computer is quantitative. In the 1960s we were a small handful, mostly of academics who had strayed in from other fields: for example, Patrick Suppes from philosophy and psychology, John Kemeny (who invented BASIC) from physics and university administration, Donald Bitzer (who developed the PLATO system) from engineering, and myself from mathematics and the study of intelligence. There were also a few entrepreneurs who lost money in premature attempts to commercialize the field. In the early 1970s we

were a larger handful. The big break came with the advent of the microcomputer in the middle of the decade. By the early 1980s the numbers of people who devoted a significant part of their professional time to computers and education had shot up from a few hundred to tens of thousands. By now it is in the hundreds of thousands, most of them teachers, although many thousands are engaged in the research and business wings of the world of educational computing.

The story that is harder to tell but also far more important to know is subjective and sociological. It concerns what these growing numbers of people think and how the development of this culture relates to wider trends in society. My overarching message to anyone who wishes to influence, or simply understand, the development of educational computing is that it is not about one damn product after another (to paraphrase a saying about how school teaches history). Its essence is the growth of a culture, and it can be influenced constructively only through understanding and fostering trends in this culture.

The first significant move toward taking understanding beyond a quantitative level was the attempt to classify the modes of use of computers in education. The title of one of the first anthologies of papers in the area provides a witty formulation that illustrates the approach. The book by Robert Taylor (professor at Columbia Teachers College and creator of the first Master's program in computers and education) was called *The Computer in the School: Tutor, Tutee, Tool.* The intention of the first and last terms of the subtitle corresponds closely enough to popular models of what computers can do in education. Examples of the uses of computers considered as tools will be familiar to everyone. A word processor is considered to be a tool; so is a program that allows one to study ecology through simulations; and so are programs that allow one to use the computer as a calculator. The term *tutor* names the most common image of the computer in education. The term *tutee,* on the other hand, refers to a metaphor I have frequently used in thinking about programming as teaching the computer. Every professor knows that a good way to learn a subject is by teaching a course on it, and I half playfully suggested that a child could get some of the same kind of benefit by "teaching," that is to say, programming, the computer.

A slightly different classification that has been so frequently used that I have not been able to identify its original author talks about "learning with the computer; learning from the computer; and learning about the computer." *With* corresponds neatly to *tool* and *from* to *tutor*. The relationship between *about* and *tutee* is less direct but still exists, in that being able to program a computer is synonymous with learning more deeply about how it works than is required by the other two modes of use.

In this chapter, however, instead of classifying ways of using computers, I look at the development of ways of thinking about their uses. I suggest a way of thinking about successive periods of their history, defining these as "classical," "romantic," "bureaucratic," and finally "modern."

Looking back, I think of the earliest period (corresponding very roughly to the 1960s) in the development of educational computing as "classical" in a sense intriguingly resonant with Webster's definition: "conformity to established treatments, taste or critical standards . . . attention to form . . . regularity, simplicity, balance, proportion and controlled emotion (contrasted with *romantic*)." There was conformity in a double sense. We each came into education from another established field and continued to conform to a set of methods, tastes, and critical standards that were a meld of the prevailing, hard-edged computer culture and our own home disciplines. At the same time, perhaps because we felt we were guests or immigrants, we structured our work in ways that did not challenge School's fundamental assumptions. Even I, who was a Yearner of long standing and the maverick of the early community, cast my ideas in what I see now as a remarkably Schoolish mold. Emotion, to continue down Webster's list of characteristics, was certainly controlled; indeed, it was not even acknowledged as a relevant category for thinking about education. The prevailing computer culture favored keeping our focus firmly on the cognitive side of education.

A look at three participants in the early educational computer culture, Suppes, Kemeny, and myself, will be sufficient to show how its "classicism" cuts across ideas and debates about modes of use of computers in education. Patrick Suppes became the intellectual father of CAI (Computer Aided Instruction), a phrase that has become synonymous with the mode of use of the computer I characterized with some polemical overstatement as using the computer to program the student. John Kemeny was one of the fathers of BASIC and therefore a pillar of support for a very different view of the computer: The student programs the computer and so makes it a tool that aids learning rather than a robot teacher that aids instruction. Thus, along one axis Suppes and Kemeny stood at opposite extremes. But on other relevant axes they were very close. They shared a virtually exclusive emphasis on the cognitive side of learning: They saw learning in terms of facts and skills to be acquired; they had no explicit concern for feelings or for personality or for development of the individual on a level that was not reducible to such specific atoms of learning. They shared an acceptance of School. They kept their views on education separate from their engagement with politics, gender, and race. In many such respects they were distinct from the spirit of the "romantic" period, which would bring hotter social issues and more "intimate" aspects of the computer to the forefront of concern. And so, on the whole, was I.

I was certainly the obstreperous maverick of the group. I quarreled with both CAI and BASIC and developed Logo as an alternative to both. But it would take me five years to understand the anticlassical implications of ideas with which I was grappling. In the meantime I found myself acting like a "person of my time" (or perhaps even like a "man of my time"—my own work has only gradually broken with what I recognize as androcentrism, and some of my feminist friends would deny that a male could ever completely break with it).

The concept of CAI, for which Suppes's original work was the seminal model, has been criticized as using the computer as an expensive set of flash cards. Nothing could be further from Suppes's intention than any idea of mere repetitive rote. His theoretical approach had persuaded him that a correct theory of learning would allow the computer to generate, in a way that no set of flash cards could imitate, an optimal sequence of presentations based on the past history of the individual learner. At the same time the children's responses would provide significant data for the further development of the theory of learning. This was serious high science.

However, from the beginning several considerations kept the approach from sitting well with me.

My gut-level response rejected the status of object given to the child by any theory of this kind. Behaviorists are fond of using the designation "learning theory" for the foundations of their thinking, but what they are talking about is not "learning" in the sense of something a learner does but "instruction," in the sense of something the instructor does to the learner.

The form in which I was best able to articulate my disagreement at that time was epistemological, that is to say, in terms of differences about the kinds of knowledge being used. Suppes's instructional theory sought to reduce what children needed to learn in mathematics to a set of precise "factlets" that could be counted and sequenced by his computer programs. In this he was not being idiosyncratic. The logician in him supported a view of knowledge as made up of precise particles; the statistician in him liked to see knowledge as particulate and therefore countable; the neobehaviorist required it to be so. What was expressed in his work was an all-embracing epistemological paradigm, which was then dominant in large sectors (and is still powerful in some sectors) of the American academic world. From my side too this paradigm was very present in the theoretical worlds from which

I came to educational endeavors—but as an obstacle to be challenged. In psychology my mentor Piaget was the most consistent (though in America Noam Chomksy had become known as the most vehement) critic of behaviorism. In artificial intelligence (AI), my work with Marvin Minsky struggled against "logic" as the basis of reasoning and against all forms of "particulate" and "propositional" representations of knowledge.

The issue comes out in a stark form by contrasting two views of Debbie. CAI is based on a diagnosis of Debbie's difficulty as a deficiency of specific items of *knowledge* about fractions and seeks to cure the problem by supplying them. I see a deficiency—or even multiple deficiencies—in *relationship:* There is debilitating weakness both in Debbie's own relationship with fractions and in the relationships among the different pockets of what knowledge she does have. As a result she is unable to take charge either of making effective use of her existing knowledge or of generating or seeking new knowledge. I pose the educational goal not as giving her factlets but as encouraging her to make connections between different elements of what she already knows: for example, intuitive knowledge about fractions, knowledge about the "real world," and knowledge about strategies of learning. Making the connections is something only Debbie can do. They have to be *her* connections.

The advocate of CAI might say, "But we have seen that if you put people like Debbie through our programs their scores will improve. The approach must be right." Perhaps her scores will improve, but it does not follow that the underlying theory is right. The question always arises: Is there another, equally likely explanation? An anecdote points to one.

I was observing a child working with a CAI program for multiplication. There was something strange going on. I had seen the child do several multiplications quickly and accurately. Then I saw him give a series of wrong answers to easier problems. It took me a while to realize that the child had become bored with the program and was having a better time playing a game of his own invention. The game required some thinking. It redefined the "correct" answer to the computer's questions as the answer that would generate the most computer activity when the program spewed out explanations of the "mistake."

I would bet this child was one of those who would become a statistic showing gain in math ability from the use of the CAI program. Would it follow that the program was in fact a good way to teach math? Yes and no! Yes, because it did, in fact, enable the child to learn; no, because it did so for a reason quite different from what the programmer intended. The issue at stake here is whether self-directed activity was better than carefully controlled programmed activity for learning math, and this child supported the self-directed alternative. A CAI salesperson might still object (though I am sure Suppes would not) that this is of no importance if the child did in fact learn. My reply to that is what I say about most learning by rote methods with or without computers: Yes, indeed, children can make a game of anything and learn through it, but if that's what we want to see happen let's say so and work hard to find contexts in which playfulness is brought out to best advantage.

The anecdote illustrates the difference between the intellectual atmosphere of Suppes's background and mine. While he was working in the tightly controlled thinking of logic, I was working in the playful atmosphere of the MIT AI Lab. Of course, neither of us denied the importance of both formal and intuitive thinking. But we saw a reversal of relationship between them. The logician sees logic as the primary kind of thinking and struggles to explain the intuitive in logical terms. Many of my colleagues in artificial intelligence argued (and some still do) that when we are doing what we think of as intuitive thought, we are still following (without knowing it) precise, logical rules—only they are not the rules we might think that we are following. This is why they are delighted whenever anyone programs a computer to do something that resembles intuitive reasoning. The computer is following definite rules, so the task, whatever it is, can be done by following rules. For me the challenge is in the other sense. The basic kind of thought is intuitive; formal logical thinking is an artificial, though certainly often enormously useful, construct: Logic is on tap, not on top. I am delighted whenever something that appeared to be formal, rule-driven behavior turns out to be something else. This is why I was so pleased with the child playing with the CAI program.

Thus Suppes and I differed quite deeply about what kind of knowledge we wanted to foster in children. A mark of authenticity in our debate is that we differed also in our own personal styles— both in how we thought and in our appreciations of how we thought.

In one of my first encounters with Suppes he had formulated the issue of styles by summing up a debate between us at a conference on the philosophy of science. I remember his words well, since they came to be emblematic for me of what I often saw as the fundamental problem of teaching: "I would rather be precisely wrong than vaguely right."

I saw this as a fundamental problem for teaching in this sense. It had been obvious to me for a long time that one of the major difficulties in school subjects such as mathematics and science is that School insists on the student being precisely right. Surely it is necessary in some situations to be precisely right. But these situations cannot be the right ones for developing the kind of thinking that I most treasure in myself and many creative people I know. This is not thinking that goes as the logician might like, from truth to truth to truth until it gets from premise to solution. The normal state of thinking is to be off course all the time and make corrections that go back sufficiently to keep going in a generally good direction. This kind of thinking is always vaguely right and vaguely wrong at the same time.

The teaching dilemma comes from the difficulty in knowing where someone else is in such a process. So how can the teacher give advice to the student?

I had devoted much effort to looking for a theory of how

teachers could do this. I now see that I had not been able to find anything very deep for reasons rather like those that blocked the teacher at my Logo workshop: I was fixated on children in School and so was looking for ways to improve the guidance process in traditional schoolwork. The breakthrough that set me on track to what would become my trademark way of using computers came when I was able to "forget the ———— children" and think about myself.

It happened on a visit to Cyprus in 1965. I was still reeling from the culture shock that came with moving (in 1963) from the University of Geneva, where there were no computers, to MIT, where I suddenly had free access to the best machines in the world. Here on this remote Mediterranean island I was feeling my first absence from a way of life in which computers were a constant presence. This in turn stirred up thoughts about how much I had learned since coming to MIT, how I had used a computer to make a breakthrough on a theoretical problem that had bothered me for some time, how concepts related to computers were changing my thinking in many different areas. Then in a flash came the "obvious" idea: What computers had offered me was exactly what they should offer children! They should serve children as instruments to work with and to think with, as the means to carry out projects, the source of concepts to think new ideas. The last thing in the world I wanted or needed was a drill and practice program telling me to do this sum next or spell that word! Why should we impose such a thing on children? What had launched me into a new spurt of personal learning at MIT wasn't in the slightest bit like the CAI programs. I became obsessed with the question, Could access to computers allow children something like the kind of intellectual boost I felt I had gained from access to computers at MIT?

In a search for good examples of what children might actually do with computers, my mind raced through my own activities, making lists of ways in which I thought I had benefited from computers and asking myself in each case whether something similar could be made available for children. For a while I simply passed over the first entry on my list: artificial intelligence, the principal interest that had brought me to MIT. "Obviously not for children." Then I remembered a conversation with Piaget a few years before in which we had engaged in playful speculation about what would happen if children could play at building little artificial minds. I had been saying that the essence of AI was to make theoretical psychology concrete. So (since concreteness is supposedly what children thrive on) in principle perhaps some elementary form of it could become a children's construction set. If psychologists could benefit from making concrete models of the mind, why shouldn't children, whose need was even greater, also benefit?

Piaget liked the image of taking one of his favorite aphorisms—"to understand is to invent"—into a new domain. In the hothouse atmosphere of the discussion in Piaget's incredibly chaotic study, we were carried away by images of children understanding thinking through playing with materials needed to invent a thinking machine, an intelligence. Neither of us thought of it as very real—it was just a scenario for a philosophical *Gedankenexperiment*. But now suddenly on a mountain in Cyprus, the idea changed for me from a philosophical speculation to a real project.

The difference came from a very concrete picture of (one version of) what people actually do when they "do AI." They select a piece of human mental activity, say, playing chess or seeing a cat; then they write a computer program that will do something similar; and finally they discuss, sometimes at very great length, whether the computer program "really" does what the human did. I had been engaged in a lot of this kind of activity and knew it had stimulated me to exciting and productive insights into human thinking. True, I did not often really think that the AI program was successful in fully imitating a person; but even when the differences were more prominent than the similarities, the discussion of the machine still produced valuable insights into how people think—and into how they do not think. It seemed plausible that doing elementary AI could give children, too, a new context for thinking about thinking. Of course I would not expect them to be able to make a program to play even poor chess, so I cast around for a simpler game and fixed on something in the family of games played with piles of matchsticks. The principle, however, could be the same. My hopeful scenario of children doing elementary AI was something as follows.

A group of children is studying the matchstick game called "Twenty-one," in which two players take turns in removing one, two, or three matches from a pile of twenty-one matches; the one who takes the last match loses. The children's immediate goal is exactly that of people making what would later come to be called expert systems: Carefully watch someone engaged in the activity you want your program to imitate, and try to come up with rules you can put into a program to make the computer act similarly. The physical side of the process did not seem important. Today the means exist for children to build a robot that would play by actually picking up sticks. I actually built one for relaxation (and because I like that kind of joke) while writing this chapter, using an extended Lego kit called Lego-Logo, which was a fallout (twenty years later!) of the very work I am describing here. In state-of-the-art present-day educational computing, the game would be played using computational objects visible as icons on a screen—the computer would play by moving the icon from the row into a bin and the human opponent by dragging it with a mouse or by using keys. Back in the 1960s we used clattering teletype machines; when we got the scenario to work, the matches were X's and the machine retyped the row after each move. The human player responded by typing a number. What seemed important was how the children would do the programming and, indeed, whether the idea ran counter to established knowledge on stages of intellectual development.

My friends in the developmental psychology business were cynical about whether anything that could significantly be called programming could be managed by children who had not yet reached the so-called formal stage of development, which means about junior high school age. I saw the question as more subtle because I was more aware of how much it would depend on what is meant by "programming." It seemed intuitively obvious that nothing good would come of trying to have third-graders or even fifth-graders make game-playing programs from scratch in any of the then current programming languages such as FORTRAN or LISP. (Had BASIC or PASCAL existed I would have included them as well.) But was this because the languages were designed for adults and presupposed some elements of mathematical sophistication, or was it inherent in the concept of programming? Indeed, is there such a thing as "the concept of programming," or is "programming" something that can be constructed in radically different ways?

One could go around in circles forever with such questions. The only sensible approach was to take a first shot at making a programming language that had a better chance of matching the needs and capabilities of younger people than the existing ones. At the time, while working at MIT, I was also doing some part-time consulting for a group led by Wally Feverzeig, head of educational technology at the research firm Bolt, Beranck, and Newman, which was working on one of the earliest attempts to teach programming in a school. The group did not need much persuasion to change its goal from trying to teach existing programming languages to developing an entirely new language. We formed a team, and the next year the first language bearing the name Logo was up and running—though few of the million or so children who work with a modern form of Logo on any school day would recognize it. We decided that it was prudent to make the first trial at the junior high level just inside the "formal" boundary; the idea was to descend to lower ages as we developed techniques for teaching and improvements to the language.

It took two years and a lot of work to get from Cyprus to a place where young people (seventh-graders) could actually do something like the scenario. Not only did they do so, they even produced an unexpected twist that made the reality more interesting than the fantasy. Rather than follow strictly in the path of the so-called "knowledge engineers" who build expert systems, these students followed in the path of psychologists who deliberately construct a series of "inexpert" systems that make the computer act like a "novice" and then pass through a progression of levels of increasing expertise.

Unsurprisingly (in hindsight!) our young students were more intrigued by what some of them called "dumb programs" than by "smart programs." It might be fun to make a program that would play impeccably and always win, but some found it more enjoyable to make one they could beat and laugh at for committing the blunders they saw their friends make. The real case exceeded my original fantasy scenario in giving rise to good talk about much more than computers and programming. In one class the use of the words *dumb* and *smart* became a subject of intense discussion triggered by an interchange in which A said B's program was dumb and B countered with something like: "It's not dumb, I did it specially like that so I could add more rules. Wait and see, it'll be the smartest! Real dumb is when you make it so you can't add anything, it can't get better." In another class, discussion led to arguments about whether these judgmental words should be applied to the program or to the programmer and ended up with a consensus: Using words like *dumb* and *smart* is what's really dumb.

B reminded me of Patrick Suppes's comment about being vaguely right or precisely wrong, by defending a strategy of deliberately designing a program that would be only vaguely right but capable of being redirected, instead of shooting for being precisely right on the first shot and risking a complete miss. In this he expressed the same thought that underlies Voltaire's maxim, "the best is the enemy of the good," which Herbert Simon, Nobel Prize–winning economist and one of the founders of AI, takes as his life motto. All three thinkers, Voltaire, Simon, and B, suggest a slant on what is really wrong with School's epistemology: the very little room it leaves for being vaguely right.

It is not merely an intolerant style of teaching or testing that is responsible for the insistence in so much of schoolwork on being exactly right. The content of the curriculum and the medium of pencil and paper are inherently biased toward a true/false–right/wrong epistemology. What B discovered was that programming is inherently biased toward evaluation not by "is it right?" but by "where can it go from here?" In this he is not alone: Many virtuoso programmers insist on starting a job by making a "quick and dirty" program that is vaguely what is wanted and then seeing how to go from there. Of course, the same is true in other (perhaps all) domains of creative work. My interpretation of such stories as B's will be that while he could have made this discovery in other domains (obviously!—many did so before computers came on the scene), programming in the right supportive context offers especially favorable conditions, and the more so the younger the discoverer.

The game of Twenty-one turned out to be simple enough to be played by programs within the grasp of seventh-graders who were indeed able to draw on the experience for discussion of strategies for thinking. Students took with gusto to making programs that would generate sentences in approximate English and through doing so came to a new kind of understanding of grammar. But something was missing, and the idea of children doing AI did not really take off until we married it, nearly twenty years later, with Lego to produce a construction set for building programmable robots. The difference between these two situations touches the heart of my story, indeed of this whole book. But I am getting ahead of myself.

At the time I was both happy and frustrated. The experiment showed that seventh-graders could learn Logo and do some of the things I had hoped to see. I don't put that down; it was a significant finding. There was no doubt that some of the students did get an intellectual boost. Several who had been "average" students became straight A students. I felt confirmed and was beginning to dream ambitiously of really making a difference in how children learn. Seventh-graders are scarcely children, however, and I felt that if contact with computers were destined to have an important effect it would be at a much younger age. Yet it was obvious to me from the texture of the work that extending it downward in age was not simply a matter of developing teaching techniques. The more I got a deep feel for what it was like to work in the language as it was and to work on the kinds of projects we had been using, the clearer it became that my psychologist friends had been right: If this is what programming means, it's not for pre-formal children. Nevertheless, I knew there had to be another way to approach the problem. It needed a radically different idea.

The idea took a while to come and an even longer while for me to recognize what it was. At first I was blocked by looking too hard for something too new in a way that often happens. Afterward you realize that you had the solution to the problem all along, but you couldn't see it because you were straining your eyes and stressing your mind looking out there into the great blue yonder. In this case I found the solution when I stopped taking myself so seriously and looking so hard for something new. The new idea came from looking in a more relaxed way at what was in hand.

I was doodling at the computer as I often do by writing little programs with no particular importance or difficulty in themselves. You could call it just playing. I don't know what such activity does for the mind, but I assume it's the same as what happens when one draws patterns or pictures with pencil on paper while thinking or listening to a lecture. What happened this time came from thinking that writing programs can be like drawing in many ways. In a way the Twenty-one program is a representation—might one say a kind of picture—of the form of a mental process, just as a pencil and paper drawing can be a representation of a physical shape. The knowledge engineer's manner of work even has something in common with the portraitist's. The artist looks at how a person appears and tries to capture features in the medium of pencil and paper or paint and canvas. The knowledge engineer looks at how a person acts and tries to capture essential features in a computational medium. These analogies quickly become strained, but they led to a shift in my perception of what was important in the Twenty-one program. Previously I would have said that what was important about the program was that it represented a kind of thinking. Now I wanted to say that what counted was that it represented something the programmer does. It didn't matter that the something was thinking; it could just as well have been walking or drawing or whatever. In fact, maybe walking or drawing would be better than playing Twenty-one; children care more and know more about these activities.

The turtle came from thinking about how on earth a child could capture in computational form something physical like drawing or walking. The answer was a yellow robot shaped rather like R2D2 and, like him, mounted on wheels. Nowadays we have much smaller robots with computers inside them. We also have turtles that exist only on a computer screen. In those days the turtle was a large object, almost as big as the children who were using it, connected by wires and telephone links to a faraway computer that filled a room. One could order it around by giving instructions in proper Logo grammar. As for words, a few were built-in (innate), and one could communicate in Logo to the computer that one wanted to define a new word. What was most remarkable was that by giving Logo the handful of new commands needed to

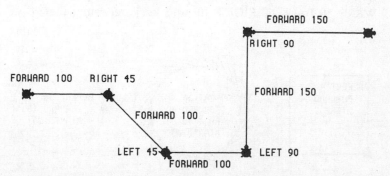

A turtle path showing commands FORWARD, RIGHT, LEFT.

control the turtle, the spirit of what could be done with it changed dramatically. Where the day before I was worrying about how to descend a year from the seventh grade, now there was an area of "baby AI" that seemed plausibly accessible to children well below school age.

We have met the essential commands. Typing FORWARD 50 causes the turtle to move in the direction it is facing a certain distance, which is to be called fifty turtle steps. Typing RIGHT 90 makes it do what in the military would be ordered by Ri-i-i-i-ght TURN! The turtle stays where it is and turns in place. If it is already moving when it gets the instruction (though this was not possible in older forms of Logo that permitted just one instruction at a time), it changes direction and continues moving in what has now become the direction it is facing.

But why should a child want to do this? And why should we be happy if a child does it?

When I saw children playing with the turtle they told me a simple elemental answer that resonated with the preoccupations I have mentioned in the last few pages. Their first step toward expressing their answer was jumping all over the turtle and demanding rides. Step 1: They clearly liked it. When the adults held back they asked one another to type commands to make the turtle move. Step 2: They took charge and used it for their own purposes. Some time later children began exercising ingenuity in giving commands that would produce interesting paths. FORWARD 50 BACK 40 RIGHT 10 (and keep repeating that) does

Combining the command REPEAT with the others.

something that some people enjoy. Step 3: It leads to invention. Step 4: It leads to the mathematical discovery that the commands FORWARD and RIGHT are a universal set in the sense that they can be combined to produce any possible path or shape.

Intellectual problems about conceptualizing thinking and the role of computers that had been troubling me began to seem tractable. I watched a boy trying to get the turtle to write his name. He wanted an A. This required developing a little theory of the geometry of an A. It is not obvious how much the turtle should turn nor how much it should advance. This is real geometry. But it differed from School geometry in a cluster of important respects. First, it was a real problem that had come spontaneously to this boy. Of course, that can happen in regular geometry too. But it is very much more likely to happen here. Second, one visibly works toward the goal by being wrong most of the time. But one can see that one is wrong and ask oneself or someone else what happened. The movements of the turtle externalize one's conception so one can think and talk about it. One can also do some of the kinds of "problem solving" that people do in the real world, such as solve another problem instead, or borrow a solution from someone else and adapt it to fit your case.

The boy trying to make an A did just that. Initially he wanted to make a 45-degree angle at the top, so he instructed the turtle FORWARD 50 RIGHT 45 FORWARD 50. This led to a shock, as you see by following the picture. What happened? He looked at the wrong angle—the angle the turtle turns is what they call the "external angle" in geometry. This kid didn't know that, but he got the idea. So after some trial and error and computing he typed

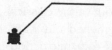

Fumbling toward an A, following a model of the A as two leaning lines with a crossbar. Successive attempts are closer.

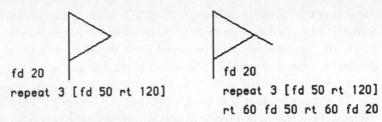

```
fd 20                          fd 20
repeat 3 [fd 50 rt 120]        repeat 3 [fd 50 rt 120]
                               rt 60 fd 50 rt 60 fd 20
```

The new model: The A is a triangle with two legs. The plan for the procedure is: Draw 1 leg (fd 20), then draw the triangle, then manuever the turtle to be in place for the other leg. To follow the steps, pay attention to the fact that repeat 3 (fd 50 rt 120) brings the turtle back to the beginning. Why 120? Because the turtle moves 360 in 3 pieces.

FORWARD 50 RIGHT 135 FORWARD 50. But now the problem was to make the cross piece. The first step is obvious: BACK 20. But how much should the turtle turn and how much should it go forward? At this point he noticed that another child was pinning up a large equilateral triangle made earlier by the turtle. You could see the "Eureka!" Why did the A need 45 degrees at the top? If Mary there could make a triangle I can too (he explained afterward that this is what he was thinking). And if I have the triangle I'll just add on extra legs and it will be an A. He still had the problem of making the triangle, but knowing that Mary had done it was a clue that helped him find out himself. In the end, there was the A.

It took another eight years before the observation of differences in style as shown by Jeff and Kevin led to the idea that computers would not simply improve school learning but support different ways of thinking and learning. But as I had watched these children my first inklings of this marked the fact that I was seeing the computer, and educational computing, move out of the classical period in which it had confirmed and strengthened old ways. Soon there would be many manifestations of the romantic period, in which conformity to old ways of thinking would be replaced by the vision of new ways.

9

• • •

Cybernetics

TELEVISION pictures of the war over Iraq gave millions of people their most vivid view of cybernetic technology, in the form of the "smart" missile, which seemed to hover like an insect before lunging into the entrance of a hangar or other building.

It is depressing to feel again that the best way to open a discussion is with a military image, but it reflects a real fact of life that has played a big role in the strategies that have guided my work. The people who forge new technological ideas do not make them for children. They often make them for war, keep them in secret places, and show them in distant views. Even when there is no deliberate concealment, there is a trend nowadays toward opaque packaging of instructive technologies. In a distant past everything a society knew might have been open to its children for use or playful imitation. Even in my youth technological objects were far more "transparent" than now. I know that it was important to my own development that I could see and at least think I understood the inner workings of trucks and cars, and eventually go through the rite of passage of tuning or even "decoking" an engine and reseating its valves. I believe that the fact that so many people grew up on farms where old tractors were kept going by ingenuity and wire and tinkering contributed to the famous American can-do mentality, and I wonder whether the opacity of modern machines is another environmental danger—a danger to the learning environment.

The physicist Richard Feynmann has written eloquently about the role in his childhood of the transparency of old-fashioned radios, and when Sherry Turkle interviewed MIT computer scientists she found that he is far from alone in having his developing mind shaped by the drama of those glowing personlike electronic tubes. Can the microchip take their place? And it is not only technical objects that have become opaque. The Bronx Botanical Garden conducted a survey that showed that many children know no prior origin for carrots than a can. I have myself known children who had not yet connected the chicken they eat with the chicken in the cute pictures in books. At their age I was used to seeing birds killed and plucked and singed, and would assert my right to remove the heart and gizzards for my first dissections there and then in the kitchen. The kitchen lore that I took in was surely richer because nothing came in cans or packages or mixes.

I do not suppose that all children were ever given full access to the ideas of any society. But at least in times of slower change, an equilibrium could be maintained between what society needed its members to know and the learning opportunities it offered (deliberately or mostly not) to its children. Since there is no reason to suppose that this is true today, and since, in any case, it is no longer acceptable that blind social forces be allowed to assign stations in life through differences in access to learning, deliberate effort is needed to bring to children knowledge that was not intended for them. School, even at its best, is too sluggish and timid to do this. In this spirit, Logo was fueled from the beginning by a Robin Hood vision of stealing programming from the technologically privileged (what I would in those early days in the 1960s have called the military-industrial complex) and giving it to children. The centerpiece of this chapter is another raid on the technologists' treasure troves.

Most people watching the missiles on TV would not have been able to give a better explanation, if asked how they worked, than that "they are programmed to do it." The booty I am after is a set of ideas (and technologies to allow children to appropriate them) that would allow a more specific answer. Of course the missiles are programmed. But they are programmed in a particular way, using specific ideas whose development has played an important role in the intellectual history of our century and whose implications might play an even bigger role in the coming one. My hope is that for anyone who has appropriated these ideas, the smart missiles will become transparent and, with them, a whole range of technologies and areas of science. In fact, these ideas are so closely interconnected in so many domains of knowledge that I shall use them here as the basis for the exercise of designing a new "subject," which I see as a more valuable intellectual area for young people than those that have been sanctified by School.

The outline of this new subject will emerge gradually, and the problem of situating it in the context of School and the larger learning environment will best be broached when we have it in front of us. Here I give a preliminary definition of the subject— but only as a seed for discussion—as *that kernel of knowledge needed for a child to invent (and, of course, build) entities with the evocatively lifelike quality of smart missiles*. If this kernel were going to be the whole subject, a suitable name would be "control engineering" or even "robotics." But the kernel is intended only as a staging area for making connections with other intellectual areas, including (among others) biology, psychology, economics, history, and philosophy. To take account of these interconnections, the subject needs a wider and less technical name. I have adopted the word that mathematician Norbert Wiener chose for the title of his highly influential book *Cybernetics: Control and Communication in the Animal and the Machine*. It is true that the word *cybernetics* failed to take firm root in English-speaking countries, but it did much better in other languages and has a better chance here for a second shot in a new, learning-oriented connotation. In any case it will do well as a provisional name for discussion in this book.

The project of developing a subject one might call "cybernetics for children" includes but goes far beyond my earlier vision of developing a framework in which children could engage in elementary artificial intelligence. The new plan shares with the older one the use of technology as a medium for representing behaviors that one can observe in oneself and other people. But the way it does this is different in three respects: The range of behaviors that can be represented will be much larger; the student's affective relationship to such work will be more intimate; and the underlying epistemology will be softer and more pluralistic.

The smart missile shows one aspect of the larger range of behaviors represented, even though it has the intelligence of a wasp rather than of a chess player. The shift from AI to cybernetics widens the focus from prototypes of behavior with a primarily *logical* flavor (such as playing chess or matchstick games) to include prototypes with a more *biological* flavor. The prototypes go beyond the human to include animals and robots, and beyond fact to include fantasy. Even very limited experiments (some of which have been carried out in collaboration with the makers of Lego) on making cybernetic construction sets for children have already allowed nine-, ten-, and eleven-year-olds to build wonderful devices that they describe as "dragons," "snakes," or "robots." Thus the children's work belongs more to what has recently been called "artificial life" than to artificial intelligence, even though many of the best projects invented by children using the construction sets are biological only in demonstrating function, rather than representing living creatures. For example, I have seen several versions of what the children called "living houses." In one such model house interior, lights go on and doors close when the outside lighting is dimmed; in another, windows and shutters close to conserve energy when the temperature falls; in yet another, the house contains "active furniture" such as a wake-up bed—a buzzer representing an alarm clock sounds at a set time, and ten seconds later the bed tilts over if the occupant is still in it.

The opportunity for fantasy opens the door to a feeling of intimacy with the work and provides a peep at how the emotional side of children's relationship with science and technology could be very different from what is traditional in School. Fantasy has always been encouraged in good creative writing and art classes. Excluding it from science is a foolish neglect of an opportunity to develop bonding between children and science. I felt that I was in the presence of something much more promising when I saw children using science and technology to try to make a dragon—*their* own dragon, which mobilized a very special kind of engagement because it came from their own fancy. By serving their intimate purposes, science and technology became much more deeply their own. In this respect the AI project was good for some children whose fantasies could be expressed by its particular kind of program, but was restrictive for those with a different kind of imagination. Like writing, and painting, and expressive multimedia, cybernetics as a creative medium has a better chance of being open enough to offer something to everyone—and to the extent that it does not, it offers better opportunities for us to work harder at extending its scope.

Turning science into "used knowledge" has epistemological implications, because it allows richer ways to think about knowledge than a true/false epistemology based on authority. Knowledge comes to be valued for being useful, for being of a kind that can be shared with others, and for matching one's personal style. In a traditional class only the most articulate and boldest students can effectively argue when a teacher rules that some way of thinking is not the right way. In an applied setting there is a better final court of appeal: "Look, it worked!" Cybernetics as a subject would share the general epistemological fallout that comes from the fact that it is used rather than simply learned, but has some specific epistemological contributions of its own.

One such contribution can be seen by looking more closely at the smart missile though the prism of Suppes's remark to me about being precisely wrong and vaguely right. It may seem paradoxical to find support in the development of weaponry for a softer and more negotiational style of epistemology against the canonical hierarchical style. After all, one thinks of the military as hierarchy par excellence and of weaponry as everything that is most macho and least negotiational. Fortunately, one of the features of the softer epistemologies is a greater tolerance for what a harder-edged epistemology would count as inconsistency and paradox.

When David used his sling to hurl a rock at Goliath's head, he was operating in the domain of the precisely right: The shot would have been worthless unless its aim was exact. The development of artillery gave value to being precisely wrong as well, for an artilleryman who knew by how much a shot overshot or fell short of the target could correct his aim to bring the next one closer. Errors became a source of information. However, the artilleryman would still be working in the domain of precise calculation. Indeed, one of the factors that drove the development of computers was the increasing complexity of the calculations needed for such work, as the range of artillery increased. With the target out of sight and the projectile traversing a whole range of temperatures and atmosphere conditions en route, calculation and information were needed—and more and more of these until the limits of the unaided human brain were exceeded. Already in the nineteenth century the production of mathematical tables in which the artilleryman could look up the settings for his shot had become a significant activity. By World War II the need had become so overwhelming that many top mathematicians were mobilized to the task, among them John von Neumann and Norbert Wiener, who became, as a direct result, leading pioneers in the emergence of computers and of computational thinking.

The development of machines to calculate better tables followed a pattern discernible in the adoption of all new technologies (including, as was noted earlier, in education): The first use of a technology always consists of striving to do better what had been done before. In this case it was still a matter of "ready, aim, fire." Once the shell was on its way, it would land where the laws of physics and the accidents of the environment would place it; no deus ex machina would make a correction. Time and the growth of ideas are usually needed before the idea of using a new technology to do something that had never been done before can even be conceived. In this case, the idea was that of making a weapon that would be brought by aim only vaguely to the right place and then turned loose to find its target. Only at this point (which was not actually reached during World War II) could one say that the technology was no longer being used to make quantitative improvements on traditional practice. Although the ultimate goal was the same, the means were more than just quantitatively different; they were epistemologically different in that they used a different way of thinking.

Traditional epistemology is an epistemology of precision: Knowledge is valued for being precise and considered inferior if it lacks precision. Cybernetics creates an epistemology of "managed vagueness." This does not mean that it has loose standards: The smart missile is expected to perform in the end even better than the traditional weapon. Cybernetics is based on a serious study of ways to make the best use of limited knowledge.

With this last statement we get a glimpse of a specific cybernetic slant in epistemology. We are still far from capturing all it has to offer, but what we are concerned with here is cybernetics as a key to learning for children. We now turn, therefore, to some examples of turtle programming that give a sense of how children can emulate the smart missile and learn by so doing about the management of uncertainty.

The turtle, it will be remembered, grew out of a concept of using programming as a medium for representing (or "sketching") one's own behavior. The geometric programs mentioned in the previous chapter did this for behaviors assumed to be predetermined without any allowance for contingencies: For example, to draw the triangle, go forward 100 units, turn right 120 degrees, and repeat this twice. To underline the difference between that mode of describing a behavior and the cybernetic mode, I cannot do better than referring to a personal learning experience that was fresh in my mind when I first thought about turtles. As a student pilot I learned to make a sharp distinction between two modes of flying from point A to point B. One is called dead reckoning. Everything is plotted before you start. You measure the distance and the direction from A to B, you study the winds, and you make allowance for how they would blow you off course if you ignored them. Once in the plane, in principle you don't even need to have a map. Set your heading at 100 degrees, fly for 75 minutes at 150 knots, and you will be there. The other method is called pilotage. In principle, you don't need to do any calculations on the ground; instead, you draw a line on the map from A to B, and as you fly you check landmarks on the ground against symbols on the map: Pass the tip of the lake . . . TV tower about a mile on the left. . . .

Turtles, as they were described earlier, were programmed in the spirit of dead reckoning. Pilotage, however, needs something else: eyes to see. This form of navigation became possible for turtles when they were fitted with sensors and so could report to the computer on interactions with their environment. Many kinds of sensors have been used in this way: A touch sensor reports to the computer that it is being touched, a light sensor reports the intensity of the light falling on it, and sound sensors, temperature sensors, and others act in similar fashion. The turtle still follows a program, but the existence of sensors permits a different relationship between the turtle's program and its movements. The program of a "geometry turtle" specified the actual movement in a geometric sense: Go forward so much, turn right so much, and so on. The program of a "cybernetics turtle" might say, in effect, "Find a light and go to it." Of course, actually "saying" this requires more than having a sensor; it requires ideas about how to use sensors to give a machine the ability to follow a goal. The program no longer follows a "blueprint," but now "emerges." As soon as children begin to use this emergent programming, they have stepped into the world of cybernetics.

The newness of the world of cybernetics becomes apparent from resistances seen in children's switch from the predetermined programming of the geometry turtle to the interactive programming of the cybernetic turtle. For example, consider how to program a turtle with touch sensors to circumnavigate a square box. Many beginners will try to use dead reckoning: Measure the box, decide that its length is 130 turtle units, and try the program REPEAT 4 [FORWARD 130 RIGHT 90]. The logic behind this is clear: We are told that computers do exactly what they are programmed to do, neither more nor less, and so the naïve programmer tells it to make exactly the movements needed to get around the box.

Excellent insights into what cybernetic thinking is about come from contemplating various flaws in this logic. First note that this is a case where being too precisely right opens one to the risk of being disastrously wrong. The program will work if, but only if, everything goes exactly according to plan. It has no margin for error. It will fail if the turtle turns a tad too soon or a tad too much. In practice, it would be almost sure to fail because not even computers—and certainly not physical objects like turtles—actually do exactly what they are expected to do. Error is a universal feature of the world, and in this case small errors can be disastrous.

Another flaw in the exact-programming approach can be appreciated only by comparison with an alternative approach, a little more like pilotage and much more in the spirit of cybernetics: that of putting oneself in the place of the turtle. One wouldn't walk around the box by taking a precise number of steps, but rather by using pilotage—or what cyberneticians would call feedback. Just so as to walk to the corner and then turn, one would at every step adjust one's course so as to keep the box a few inches to the left.

If one felt oneself too close, one would turn away slightly to the right; if one were too far, one would turn slightly to the left. This can easily be translated into a program that repeats over and over the following cycle of instructions:

TEST LEFT-TOUCH   ⟵ This causes the touch sensor to report *either*

IFYES [RIGHT 2]   ⟵ bumping the box, so turn away a little, *or*

IFNO [LEFT 2]   ⟵ losing the box, so turn toward it a little, *then*

FORWARD 2   ⟵ take a step

The reader may ask why the number 2 was chosen. The wonderful answer is that the program would work with 5 or 1 or 0.5 in place of 2. As long as the turtle turns ("vaguely") a little left or a little right and moves a little forward, it will get around the box.

The most remarkable feature of this program is its vagueness as to the size and shape of the box. The size of the box does not show in the program, and this is a strength because it means that the program will work for a box of any size. Even more remarkably, the size of the angle to be turned at each corner does not show either, which means the program will work for an object of any shape as well as any size!

Nobody who has seen both approaches (let's call them for the moment the geometric and the cybernetic) ever has any doubts about which is better for this job. The geometric approach is precarious and particular. Even if it does work for the box, it will fail if tried on, say, a circular object. The cybernetic approach is robust and very general: It will work every time on almost any object to be circumnavigated. Yet in my experience, many if not most people who meet the problem cold will prefer the geometric approach.

Why is this? One factor, of course, is lack of experience with cybernetic situations. But I think that a more powerful factor is a supervaluation of the "abstract" and "mathematical" acquired from the general culture and especially from School. By the same token, the success of the cybernetic approach contributes to the revaluation of the concrete. In this case, *concrete* surely means putting yourself in the place of the turtle as you imagine it going around; and doing so with an open mind should raise doubts about the geometric approach as well as heuristically suggesting the cybernetic one.

The "vague" cybernetic approach is, moreover, universal— that is, it will work with any kind of sensor. For example, think of a turtle with a light sensor on each side. The problem is to program the turtle so that if a light is placed in its field, it will go to it.

A classical programming approach would suggest an exact imitation of the dead-reckoning procedure for airplanes: Split the problem into two parts, first determine where the light is, and then go there. Putting this plan into practice needs some mathematical technique which I will omit since what is most interesting here is the extraordinary simplicity of the cybernetic method. The key fragment of a workable program is.

TEST LEFT-SENSOR ← RIGHT-SENSOR ←	Is light stronger on left?
IFYES [LEFT 10]	←	Turns turtle toward the light
IFNO [RIGHT 10]	←	Ditto
FORWARD 5	←	In any case, move forward a little

What is interesting here is again the extreme vagueness of the turtle's knowledge about where the light is located. If the light is anywhere to the left, the turtle turns left; if it is anywhere to the right, it turns right. If the light is too near the center, the turtle makes what is effectively a random turn one way or the other. Yet this will eventually bring the turtle to the light—not approximately to the light, but right there!

A saying tells us that the chain is no stronger than its weakest link. In this it is not expressing a universal truth but the ideology of linear hierarchical thinking. Many classical computer programs, many mechanisms, and many logical arguments are constructed in such a way that the whole will work only if every part is exactly right. A fundamental tenet of cybernetics is that living systems do not work like that; and, moreover, the principles by which they escape the apparently inexorable truth of the saying are of great importance not only for understanding biology but for designing technologies and for conducting social and personal life. Much of the attraction of early cybernetics came from the apparent magic of systems that worked much better than their parts. Claude Shannon, the founder of modern information theory, had constructed amazingly efficient error-correcting codes: Even if a noisy cable caused an extra blip here and there, a decoding device at the receiving end could reconstruct the message. Frank Rosenblatt had built a kind of computer called a perceptron which had the wonderful ability of continuing to work with only gradual deterioration of performance as one plucked out its parts at random. (Don't try that on your PC.) Warren McCulloch, the polymath who should be counted with Wiener as co-founder of cybernetics, wrote eloquently about how our brains keep functioning recognizably even though tens of thousands of neurons die every day, and how pouring such chemicals as alcohol into the system changes the behavior of the individual cells far more than the behavior of the whole. And, of course, if our light-seeking turtle makes a mistake every now and then it will follow a different path but still get to the goal—in fact, it will eventually get there even if its decision about which side gets more light is randomly wrong most of the time.

The purpose of noting that a system can be more reliable than its components is not a blanket exoneration of mindless sloppiness. If one wired the turtle so that right and left were interchanged, the program we wrote would never bring it to the light—quite the contrary, it would be photophobic and flee light.

On the other hand, a fifth-grader with a little cybernetic experience could write a different and not very much more complicated program that would adapt to such mistakes in wiring. Cybernetics, in fact, is full of principles of adaptation to a world that can never be exactly predicted or completely controlled. These principles have names like "redundancy," "systemic thinking," "statistical trend," "self-organizing system," and "feedback." Most of what follows applies to the other principles as well. Here, however, I focus on feedback, taken as an example both to show what kind of idea cybernetics breeds and, in particular, to justify the choice of cybernetics as knowledge to be made available to children.

Two extreme answers to the question of choosing such knowledge must be rejected. The extreme position on the conservative side is to follow what is already in the school curriculum: There is already more there than children seem to be able to learn; reformers will do better to improve teaching what is there than aggravating the situation by quixotically proposing new subjects. But on my reckoning, the fraction of human knowledge that is in the curriculum is well under a millionth and diminishing fast. I simply cannot escape from the question: Why that millionth in particular? In any case, plenty of people are busy polishing the established millionth (or billionth or whatever it actually is), so the few of us who seem willing to explore elsewhere will not be missed.

The radical answer is that we should make all knowledge available so as not to impose our own prejudiced views on the next generation. In my discussion of Jennifer and the Knowledge Machine I myself proposed something like that in a long-term approach to factual knowledge. Yes, I do think that children should and one day will have free access to knowledge about Africa and Tibet as well as America and Europe, about giraffes and elephants as well as cats and dogs, about Shaka and Dingaan and their descendants as well as King George and his descendants.

If I could make such a Knowledge Machine, I would. But no one person can. The only way to approach its ever coming into being is through systemic thinking. The crucial question for me is: What can I do now to speed the necessarily social process that can lead to the eventual development of the Knowledge Machine or, rather, of the better idea that is sure to take us all by surprise when it emerges? My answer is to follow my intellectual sensors and try as I go to articulate the criteria that draw me to cybernetics as a choice for the billionth of human knowledge that is as much as one person can try to make directly available.

One criterion shouts for attention: Is there a billionth that will be especially effective in opening doors to much larger areas and giving people more freedom to make personal choices? To see whether a concept is capable of playing this role, we must see whether it possesses the qualities of appropriability and generativity. The meaning of these concepts will emerge from a discussion of why feedback qualifies as a mathetically powerful idea by its strength on both counts.

Evidence for the appropriability of the concept is that this has already happened on a large scale. Books on wildflowers use a vocabulary of "escaping from cultivation" and becoming "naturalized." It is not hard to trace a route by which the word *feedback* escaped from cultivation in the esoteric language of such people as radio engineers, who used it to describe a technique for stabilizing an amplifier by "feeding" a fraction of the output "back" to the input. By the 1940s the concept of feedback had developed into a form that will be the theme of this chapter and was gaining recognition as important in many branches of engineering and also in physiology.

The excitement around this early form of cybernetics (which would not be called that until 1948) drew in a number of people whose interests were in neither engineering nor physiology. Typical and most influential of these was anthropologist Gregory Bateson, who saw that these ideas could be important in understanding human behavior. Bateson became a central figure on the psychological scene in the 1960s; and through this channel, ideas, and certainly words, from cybernetics spread into popular cultures that were even further removed from anything technical, indeed, that were profoundly antitechnical. Thus the stage was set for a general amnesia about the technological origin of the word that became very clear to me when I conducted an informal poll, asking acquaintances what the word *feedback* suggested to them.

Most spoke about responsiveness in human relationships. A teacher spoke about the need to "get feedback" from her class. A friend who had experience with family therapy spoke about how spirals of a worsening relationship come about when a person's anger gives rise to behaviors in other people that aggravate that person's anger. This use of the word is closer to the technical origin than the teacher's, but my friend was not aware of any such connection and was quite surprised by the fact that the spiral buildup of anger could be modeled physically by placing the microphone of a public address system near the loudspeaker and turning up the volume control: A little sound whispered into the microphone produces a sound from the loudspeaker that "feeds back" into the microphone. If what feeds back is even ever so slightly louder than the original whisper, a self-perpetuating and self-augmenting process is created, and very soon the room is filled with an ear-splitting whine. The phenomenon is called "positive feedback." Whenever a state of a system, say, the anger level or the sound level, produces effects that augment that state, there is positive feedback; and when there is positive feedback, the anger or the sound or whatever it is will grow until something snaps or blocks.

Another sign of the concept's appropriability is the ease with which it is taken up in humor. One of my students reported an example of a real event that shows this feature. A couple, let's say A and B, share a bed with an electric blanket. In this case the blanket provided separate dials for the two sleepers, so that the heat could be separately adjusted on each side of the bed. At least, that was what was intended. On one occasion the dials got crossed, so that A, on the left side, held the dial that controlled the heater on the right side, and vice versa. A woke up feeling cold, and turned up the dial expecting to get more heat. But the extra heat was generated on B's side, and B, feeling hotter, turned the heat down. A became even colder and turned the heat even farther up. So B got even hotter and turned the heat even farther down. Now A was really shivering and turned the heat to maximum. The effect is to raise B's side to roasting temperature and reduce A's temperature even more. If they didn't know it before, A and B certainly knew something about positive feedback after they sorted this one out.

Negative feedback, which is more useful and more intriguing, does the opposite. The simplest model is a thermostat that controls heat and air-conditioning. Set the dial to 70. If the room gets hot, that is to say, above 70, the thermostat starts the air-conditioning. The feedback is called negative, because the state of heat produces an effect that will reduce heat, and the state of cold produces an effect that will reduce cold. In one sense no mechanism could be more simple. Yet many have been impressed by the quality this system shares with living beings: It acts as if it had a purpose, as if it is determined to keep the temperature at the set level of 70 degrees.

Some people have engaged in philosophical discussion about whether a thermostat really has purposes or goals. To me, this smacks of rather futile wordplay if it is pursued in a spirit of seeking the ultimate truth one way or the other, though there are ways to pursue it that could make for valuable discussion among children of epistemological and psychological principles. But the pragmatic discovery that the principle can be used to design machines that behave as if they are following goals is basic to modern technology. The fact that the thermostat seems to have the goal of keeping the temperature in the house constant does not stir me particularly. But however much I know about how such things work, I still find it evocative to see a Lego vehicle follow a flashlight or turn toward me when I clap my hands. Is my reaction a streak of residual metaphysics? Is it because the little thing seems somehow betwixt and between? I know that it isn't alive, but it shares just enough with living beings to excite me—and many others too. Whatever the reason, such things are intriguing and making them is an exciting way to engage with an important body of knowledge.

What makes the principle even more remarkable is that it is also generative: It can be used to understand many situations, and some in very surprising ways. It is rich in intellectual jokes and comic or paradoxical situations.

We already had one comic situation with the double electric blanket. In the same spirit, here is a tricky question: How can you use a piece of ice to heat a room? A better quiz question than yet another repetition of calculating the volume of a gas if it is heated 20 degrees. Well, the answer is: You put it on the thermostat! What does that do? It makes the thermostat think the room is cold, so it turns on the heat. As long as the ice is there, the heat will go full blast. The room will become as hot as the heating system can make it.

Our body temperature is maintained by a thermostat that is more complex than the simple one that keeps the room comfortable. But its principle has to be the same: Somehow the system must know whether the temperature is above or below the set level—in this case, about 97 degrees Fahrenheit. If the temperature is less than the set level, a process is put into motion that will raise the temperature—for example, shivering and constricting the blood vessels near the skin. The movement of the muscles generates heat, and the vasoconstriction reduces its loss. If the temperature is above the set value, a process is put into motion that will decrease it—for example, panting, sweating, and dilation of superficial blood vessels.

That much is easy to understand. But here's a trick question. When you have a fever you are hot, and you also often shiver. Yet shivering is a reaction to cold. How come you are hot and shiver?

The question is a nice example of an engaging paradox. The answer comes from noticing that being hot and being cold are relative. When you have a fever you are hot compared with the normal temperature. But you may not be hot compared with the set level: A fever makes you hot by the equivalent of raising the thermostat setting so that the normal mechanisms for adjusting body heat operate to keep you at the new set temperature.

Another phenomenon that is explained by the body setting a "goal level" for a feedback mechanism is one that frustrates dieters in their attempt to lose weight. It appears that the body "tries" to maintain a certain weight level by adjusting the rate at which energy is dissipated. If this weight level is not the one that the person desires, a conflict of wills is created between the person's goals and that of the feedback mechanism governing weight: When body weight falls below the level set for the feedback system, the mechanism sets processes in motion to increase weight or at least slow the fall.

Since it is not possible to discuss everything at once I glossed over a difficulty we had encountered when we first tried to work with the touch-sensor turtle. Pilot experiments about twenty years ago showed that these ideas were accessible to children. Fifth-graders could carry out assignments requiring the use of feedback, but for most children these stayed on the level of assignments, in marked contrast to the way in which their graphics activities took on a life of their own.

My first shot at fixing the problem is worth mentioning here even though it led up a blind alley, since it illustrates an educational developer's knee-jerk response to a difficulty. In addition, it shows how hard it was for me to grasp the significance of what was already being learned from the experience with graphics. Our problem seemed to be much like the one we faced in the first Logo classes. This observation led to a blind alley in the following way. At that time, we had solved the problem by creating the turtle, so we should solve this one by making more creatures. This would give children more choice and so generate more enthusiasm. The upshot was that we made a range of new computer-controlled objects, of which the most memorable were a pneumatic worm and a wooden puppet. We and some of the children had fun, but all this was beside the point.

The real problem was that I was still thinking in terms of how to "get the children to do something." This is the educator's instinctive way of thinking: How can you get children to like math, to write wonderfully, to enjoy programming, to use higher-order thinking skills? It took a long time for me to understand in my gut, even after I was going around saying it, that Logo graphics was successful because of the power it *gave to* children, not because of the performance it *got from* them. Drawing was something already rooted in their culture; with the computer they took something that was already theirs into new (don't say "better") directions. For that matter, dealing with images on screens was already in their lives and important to them; the graphics turtle offered them new ways to relate to these images. Representing behaviors by programming a cybernetics turtle did not have roots in the lives of most children.

Nevertheless I had a hunch that cybernetics was a world children would like and profit from. I continued fretting over the problem. Though the solution was simple enough in concept when it came, it came slowly and took many years to implement. The point was to give up trying to entice children into my cybernetic world of turtles and instead to put cybernetics into their world. This idea, which took shape in the mid-1980s, is what led to my collaboration with Lego. Children love constructing things, so let's choose a construction set and add to it whatever is needed for them to make cybernetic models. They should be able to make a turtle with motors and sensors, and have a way to write Logo programs to guide it; or if they wished to make a dragon or a truck or a wake-up bed, they should have that option too. They should be limited only by their imaginations and technical skills. In early experiments with this concept, the motors and sensors had to be connected to a computer via an interface box. More recently we have built computers small enough to go into the models themselves. The difference feels substantial; now the intelligence really is in the model rather than in an out-of-scale computer. Besides, the models can now be autonomous. They can range far afield without an umbilical cord. It all makes it more real.

However, the biggest shift in the development of the Lego-Logo toward being "real" in the lives of children will come when the activity moves out of school into the home. Looking toward the future, it seems obvious that children will grow up building cybernetic constructs as fluently as they now build cars and houses or train-track circuits. Only then will cybernetic thinking really become part of their culture.

This fact goes a long way toward answering the two questions about Lego-Logo most often asked by parents and teachers: What will they learn from it? And won't it favor boys over girls? In my own mind, the answers to both questions are rather different from what most questioners are driving at. The first question concerns what piece of the school curriculum is being learned, but I attach most importance to such issues as children's relationship with technology, their idea of learning, their sense of self. As for the gender issue, I am thinking more about how in the long run computational activities will affect gender than about how gender will affect the activities. For gender is not mainly a matter of biology, it is a social construct; and the degree of change I anticipate in children's lives will surely one way or another result in a different construct. What I do think is important is for women to participate in forming the computer culture of the future.

But having made these remarks in a spirit of provoking reflection, I turn to the more immediate kind of question, giving an example of a very specific kind of learning through Lego-Logo. Sooner or later in building objects with Lego, students run into the need for gears. Their work provides good examples of material that overlaps with School science and math, and of an alternative style applied to these subjects—instead of a formal style that uses rules, a concrete style that uses objects.

The motors in the construction set turn at a high speed with low torque. A car built by attaching these motors directly to the wheels will go very fast, but will be so underpowered that the slightest slope or obstruction will cause it to stall. The solution to the problem with Lego cars is the same as that adopted by designers of real cars: Use gears. Yet in order to use them effectively, children need to understand something about gear ratios. This in turn brings with it a cluster of ideas such as force, torque (the physicist's measure of the "force" of turning), and mechanical advantage.

An aspect of this knowledge, which is on the cutting edge of learning for children of elementary school ages, is its rational, or relative, aspect. If a small gear drives a larger gear, the larger gear will turn more slowly and with greater torque. It is the relative and not the absolute size of the two gears that counts. But many children at this age, mainly boys, tend to reason as if the size of only one gear matters—as if they were following a set of rules such as "large gears are slow and strong" and "small gears are fast and weak." (See illustration on page 200.) Without the notion of relative size, such rules fail. Other children, predominantly girls, are less articulate and more physical in their explanations. They squirm and twist their bodies as they try to explain how they figure things out, and they get the right answer.

Theorists who look at intellectual development as the acquisition of increasingly sophisticated rules would say that children run into problems if the rules they have built are not yet good enough. The idea of concrete thinking enables us to consider a different kind of theory. Our observations suggest that the children who did well did not have better rules, but a tendency to see things in terms of relationships rather than properties. They had access to a style of reasoning that allowed them to imagine themselves "inside the system." They used a relationship to the gears to help them think through a problem.

This "reasoning from within" may not be adequate for all problems with gears, but for the kind of problem encountered by the children in our project it was not only adequate but much less prone to the errors produced by a too simple set of rules.

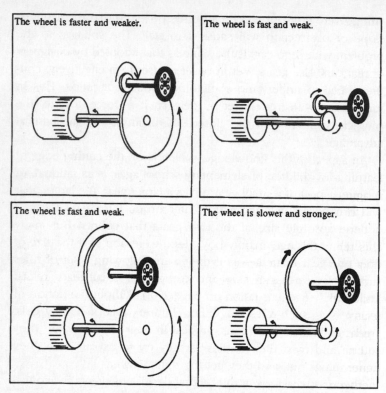

A schematic representation of a gear train between a motor and the wheels of a vehicle.

Relational, concrete thinking puts you at an advantage: You do not suffer disaster if the rule is not exactly right. This suggests, though all this is still highly speculative, that there may here be pockets of physical scientific knowledge that are more accessible to girls than to boys.

I defined *bricolage* as a style of organizing work that can be described as negotiational rather than planned in advance—what Warren McCulloch called "heterarchical" rather than hierarchical. The example of the children and their gears serves to introduce another characteristic displayed by many *bricoleur* programmers, which Turkle and I have called "proximality," or closeness to the object. A programmer like Kevin is closer to his computational objects than someone like Jeff. Like the children who "reasoned from within" with the gears, Kevin psychologically places himself in the same space as the screen turtles. He experiences his spaceship as tangible, sensuous, and tactile. He is down there, in with the sprites, playing with them like objects in a collage. Kevin talks about these objects using gestures of hand and body that show him moving with and among them. In speaking of them, he uses language such as "I move here."

I chose Kevin, a boy, to illustrate "reasoning from within" in order to avoid overstating the correlation with gender of behaviors that are, however, more characteristic of girls. The general idea I want to stress is that the relationships among gender, technology, and hard science take on new aspects in a context where children can work intimately with physical computational objects. This gives cybernetics another claim to be a new subject that will open new intellectual domains to children.

I next turn to some more sophisticated concepts in the same general area as cybernetics. To begin with, consider an experiment reported by my colleague Mitchel Resnick using a version of Logo that he calls *Logo (Star Logo), which, among other things, allows for very large numbers of turtles. In his Ph.D. thesis, Resnick talks about a "centralized mindset," which leads people to postulate a directing agent, rather than look for explanations as emergent from decentralized interactions.

Two high school students who had recently received their driver's licenses decided to use *Logo to show cars moving on a highway. The students started by creating several dozen turtles, each representing a car, and then wrote a very simple program for each car. The program consisted of two simple rules. If a car sensed another car ahead of it, it slowed down. If it didn't sense another car, it speeded up. With this simple program the students did not expect much to happen, but when they ran it, the cars bunched into a realistic-looking traffic jam. The students were surprised to see such a complex pattern forming from their simple little program. Indeed, the program provided a striking example of self-organization: The cars seemed to form themselves into a pattern without any centralized control. The jam just emerged from the interactions among the individual cars, but the students felt there must be a "cause."

This same idea comes up in all areas of science. In biology, ants organize themselves into trails to look for food; birds organize themselves into flocks so as to migrate; on longer times scales, genes organize themselves into new creatures. It is worth noting that the students appreciated the self-organizing nature of the traffic jam only because they had written the programs themselves. Had they been using a packaged simulation, they would have had no way of knowing the elegant simplicity of the programs underlying the jam.

When the students started watching the traffic jam, they were in for another surprise: The traffic jam moved backward. They found this behavior counterintuitive. How could a traffic jam move backward when all of the cars within it were moving forward? This behavior highlighted an important idea: Emergent structures often behave very differently than the elements that compose them. This idea is true not only for traffic jams but for a much wider range of phenomena, including waves. Ideas about waves are notoriously difficult for beginning students to grasp. One reason is that waves are often presented in unmotivated contexts (such as moving along a string) or as a difficult mathematical formalism (a differential equation). The *Logo traffic program provided a much more meaningful introduction to such problems, especially since the students had recently received their driver's licenses. Moreover, the waves were generated by an accessible formal system, a set of simple computer programs. Furthermore, since the students wrote the programs themselves, they were able to manipulate the programs to explore many different wavelike phenomena.

The examples of the traffic jam and the gears show how cybernetic ideas connect with concepts in the physical as well as in the biological sciences on both the advanced and the elementary levels. In this way, cybernetics possesses a combination of appropriability with richness of scientific connection. In addition to its connections with classical science, cybernetics is closely related to another modern area of knowledge often known as "systems theory," which in turn is closely connected with ways of thinking that are prominent in economics, ecology, and the study of evolution. The same kind of thinking that went into programming and then understanding the traffic situation can be applied with the same ease to situations in which there are several kinds of objects, for example, two species of animals, one a predator and the other its prey, and a plant that is eaten by the second animal species. In a few hours' work a junior high school student can set up a microworld with populations of the two animals and the plant, by specifying how much each animal eats per unit time, and how frequently all three species breed and die.

I conclude by saying something about the implications of this kind of work for the concept of programming. It is an adage (attributed to Lady Lovelace in the nineteenth century) that a computer does exactly what it is told to do, neither more nor less. But a deep ambiguity inherent in this statement becomes apparent if one compares the two turtles moving around a square box, one following a geometric and the other a cybernetic program, that were mentioned earlier. Are they doing exactly what they were "told" to do? If "telling" means actually writing it explicitly in the program, then one could say that the geometric turtle was "told" to go around the box. What the cybernetic turtle was told, however, looks very different; in fact, it might need some thinking to decide that its program would make it go around the box. There is a distance between what it was told and those aspects of its behavior that interest the programmer. In other cases the distance been program and result can be even greater. An example that is familiar to anyone who has done much Logo is the program that draws a circle by doing REPEAT 360 [FORWARD 1 RIGHT 1]. Was the turtle told to draw a circle? If one says yes, one must say that it was told this in a very odd way.

Earlier, I made a distinction between dead reckoning, or blueprint programming, and pilotage, or emergent programming. In the next chapter I shall use the language of blueprint and emergent programming to talk about economics and other "systemic" situations. I think it will appear that experience in the kinds of work discussed in this chapter will prepare young minds for the issues discussed there.

10

● ● ●

What Can Be Done?

WHEN one is overwhelmed, as everyone must be from time to time, by a sense that School is too firmly implanted ever to change, it is helpful to contemplate the political changes across the globe that were until recently considered quite impossible. The events in what we used to call the Soviet bloc are the most dramatic, but developments in South Africa, Chile, and Central America are in the same class.

The sight of crowds demolishing the Berlin wall, or of Nelson Mandela sitting at a negotiating table with Frederik de Klerk, is a potent antidote to any tendency to say, "It can't happen." But the way these things did happen is sobering as well as heady. A closer look carries many lessons about the pain and difficulty of changing a large, stable, well-rooted social structure. One of the most important of these is about how a system defends itself against recognizing the depth of its problems and the need for fundamental change.

Mikhail Gorbachev, whose name has deservedly become emblematic of change, is also one of history's most interesting examples of resistance to change. Even as he ushered in previously unthinkable reforms, he continued to pay allegiance to the ideas on which the system was founded, and renounced the Communist party only when he was on the verge of being renounced himself. His slogan of perestroika (which literally means "restructuring") became synonymous with a policy of struggling to reform a system in serious crisis without calling in question the foundations on which it was built. It should be clear by now that I see most of those who talk loudly about "restructuring" in education in much the same light—though few of them have the courage to carry the reforms as far in their realm as Gorbachev did in his. In their case a more appropriate phrase than "restructuring" might be "jiggering the system."

The analogy between perestroika and education reform would be instructive even if it went no further than highlighting these general features of change and resistance to change. But there is more. Using the language of system dynamics developed earlier, the problems of both the old Soviet Union and School can be described in terms of a conflict between tightly and emergently programmed systems.

One of the key arguments used to justify the command economy is that a tightly programmed, highly planned economic system would necessarily be more efficient than one that operates though myriads of individual, uncoordinated decisions. In the Soviet Union this philosophical position was translated into a vast organization known as Gosplan, whose task was to program the entire economy in the tightest possible way. Every detail of every product was included in a master plan. For example, the plan would decree how many nails would be produced in the entire Soviet Union, where they would be made, how they would be distributed, and at what price they would be sold. The planners would know how many nails to make because they also decided how many would be made of each product that used nails. What was true of nails was true of everything else, resulting (theoretically) in a fully rational economy with no waste—how much more sensible, it was argued, than the chaos of the capitalist market economy, where every Tom, Dick, and Harry could decide to make nails, or not to make them.

We encountered this same argument earlier, in the case of the "cathedral model" for education. The construction of a great Gothic cathedral (or any other large building) is a process that does require tight programming. It is not plausible that a cathedral would emerge from allowing workers to take independent actions of carving and placing blocks of stone. Careful planning by a skilled architect is obviously needed. The cathedral model for education applies the same principle to building knowledge structures. The curriculum designer is cast in the role of a "knowledge architect" who will specify a plan, a tight program, for the placement of "knowledge bricks" in children's minds. This is not very different from the argument for a Gosplan approach to economics.

Throughout this book I have developed concrete examples and abstract arguments to show that the Gosplan/cathedral form of tight programming is wrong as a general approach to education.
The earlier discussion of blueprint programming and emergent programming supported this position indirectly by showing that even in simple physical situations, the argument for the advantage —
of precise blueprint programming is not universally valid. Some-
thing as simple as programming a turtle to circumnavigate a rectangular box was easily done using an emergent approach, while it was difficult or even impossible to achieve by the blueprint method. The failure of the Soviet-style command economy adds one more nail to the coffin of the idea that this method is ultimately superior. Important cases where some element of blueprinting is essential are the occasional exceptions rather than the model for how a project should be carried out.

One cannot argue that the Soviet failure proves that a command economy cannot work, since its particular implementation was associated with so many other socially destructive policies. However, specific flaws in the operation of the system do suggest holes in the argument for its ultimate rationality. Consider the following schematic version of a kind of situation that had become endemic.

The Ilyanova factory was required by the plan to produce 100 tons of nails. The director had the idea of making oversized nails and produced 150 tons, so that he was rewarded with a bonus for 150 percent achievement of the plan, even though nobody could use such large nails. It is really irrelevant whether the director's idea was brilliantly fraudulent or foolishly sincere; the absurdity of the system is brought out by the fact that every nail factory could fulfill its plan and at the same time there could be a national shortage of nails.

Of course, under any system some people make fraudulent or foolish decisions. The relevant difference between the command economy and a market economy lies in the elbow room for other people to step into the breach: If the nail makers do not supply the nails for which there is a demand, sooner or later someone will realize that there is money to be made by creating a new nail factory. Thus initiative is widely distributed in the system and keeps it going through the operation of countless small and large feedback loops, working on the principles discussed in the previous chapter. What is typical of emergently programmed systems is that deviations from what was expected do not cause the whole to collapse but provoke adaptive responses.

I would not like to argue that we actually live in a fully sensible economic system—far from it. For many people the restrictions of poverty, prejudice, and our own forms of bureaucracy make a mockery of the concept of free enterprise. Even the economically powerful are constrained by limits to rationality. For example, the emphasis in American business on quarterly profits instead of looking at the real health of the company introduces an element reminiscent of judging success by counting nails. Nor would I like to argue that the Soviet system offered no opportunities at all for sensible initiatives; the fact that it survived as long as it did suggests that it did not fully conform to its own self-destructive ideal. Thus the comparison is not one of snow white and jet black.

What I do want to argue is that while our economic system,

with all its faults, is above a threshold of functionality and theirs was below it, our education system falls on the same side of the line as the Soviet economy. We are living with an educational system that is fundamentally as irrational as the command economy and ultimately for the same reason. It does not have the capacity for local adaptation that is necessary for a complex system even to function efficiently in a changing environment, and is doubly necessary for such a system to be able to evolve.

What this means will be appreciated more concretely by looking at proposals for education reforms that fail in systemic thinking. A good example is the plan with the grandiose title "America 2000," announced by George Bush so as to make good on his campaign promise to become "the education president." My discussion is not intended as a partisan attack on Bush; the flaws in thinking are, in more or less severe forms, almost universal in contemporary educational thinking.

The Bush plan was extraordinarily reminiscent of the Soviet style of "solving" problems by decree. Bush announced that by the end of the century American students will be the best in the world. The lynchpin of his proposals for achieving this was to institute a national system of tests. If this happened, he seemed to hope, Americans would no longer have to be embarrassed by reading that their children scored seventeenth in an international survey of science knowledge, or wonder whether there is after all any truth in the statement made by a Japanese politician in 1992 that American workers are lazy and ignorant. He could point to our schools' productivity in test scores as the Soviet propagandists could point to their economy's output of nails.

Defining educational success by test scores is not very different from counting nails made rather than nails used. There was no hint in Bush's education plan of any specific theory of what might be wrong with the present situation on the level of underlying mechanisms. His remedies were the remedies the bureaucratic mind proposes indiscriminately for every situation: Issue orders; tighten controls. Weakness in results can mean only that people are lazy and that a good system of tests will expose them.

But we can learn better by looking, for example, at Maria, the girl who placed the flashing light in her Lego house. She was certainly typical of contributors to the low U.S. rating on international tests. Quite likely she still is: It is improbable that her isolated experience with Lego-Logo did more than provide a hint at how she might develop first a taste and then an intuitive sense for things scientific and technological. Of course, the experience may have planted a seed for future development, though even if this were so I would not be at all sure that the change would show up as a higher score on a national test of science knowledge. In any case, whatever good came of the experience had little to do with whether there is or is not a national test; it had everything to do with giving her an unusual opportunity to develop a healthy personal relationship with science.

Indeed, if testing of the kind that Bush seemed to have in mind did have any effect on Maria at all, it would be negative. At least three different mechanisms would contribute to this. Nervousness about being tested on subjects that feel alien is the surest way to turn off what little interest a girl like Maria might have in science. On a more substantive level, tests would reinforce in her a very wrong and distasteful image of science as a list of facts to be memorized like a ritual. Furthermore, Maria would not be the only one to be influenced in these ways: Nervousness about the test could make the teacher reticent about spending time on any but the testable aspects of science.

What would draw Maria and millions of others like her toward science, however, is offering them broader opportunities to appropriate it in a personal way. As such new opportunities are developed, it will be valuable to develop means to allow students, parents, and teachers to get a sense of how they are doing. Perhaps this will be called "testing," though the connotation of that word is so bad that something better should be invented. But whatever it is called, such a feedback mechanism must come in the wake and not in the lead of new approaches to learning: A system of tests based on old models of learning will at best reinforce those models and inhibit the development of new directions.

Suppose—since there is no point in even thinking about reforming education if we preclude success—the United States were to take a global lead in developing an approach to science education based on systems theory, or on allowing each child to become deeply involved in one personally selected branch of traditional science. Suppose also, as would be likely, that even if one or two countries were to join us or be ahead of us, most countries would lag behind and continue in the old paths. Under these conditions, our children might well rank poorly in international competition on old-fashioned tests: If the tests are inherited from the past or imitated from the rest of the world, they will inhibit us from moving forward except at the pace of the rest of the world. In fact, this might well mean not moving at all, since a change may have to reach a critical size in order to take place. The way to be first, therefore, is not to play catch-up but to take the lead in new directions.

This is not to deny the need for a system of indicators of how well things are working. What was wrong with Bush's plan is that the test is not part of a self-correcting mechanism. Consider, for example, the light-seeking turtle. It used the principle of negative feedback, which by its nature implies some indicator of deviation from an intended state. Indeed, the key idea in designing the turtle for emergent programming was the selection of a suitable indicator. The design discussed in the text rejected the more obvious indicator of actual distance from the light in favor of the less "exact" indicator of deviation to left or to right. This indicator did not reflect how much progress had been made, but it did show the direction to go in order to make more progress. Likewise, any teacher watching Maria would have easy access to such an indicator and could put it to much better use than a measure simply of how much science the student knows. The teacher would see that

Maria was becoming engaged with a particular corner of technological work and could conclude that she should be encouraged
to go further in that direction. Indeed, Maria could draw this
conclusion herself! The educational flaw did not come from the
lack of indicators of directions to take but from the fact that School
provided only one direction and perforce she took it. After her
individual experience she went back to the impersonality of the
curriculum.

In the same way, in the case of the nail factory, the command
system and the market system both use an indicator of nail production—a test. In one case the test measured conformity to the
plan, and we saw how that worked in a situation that is not as
aberrant as it might seem. In the other case the test is the price of
nails, which would respond to a shortage by going up and thus
encourage producers to make more nails or potential producers to
come into the nail business.

In short, thinking about tests points up the real problem of our
education system: the lack of flexibility in making sensible responses to what appropriate tests might reveal. The problem is to
break away from School's uniformity.

Here, too, the plan proposed by the Bush administration provides insight into how not to think about the issue. Bush and his
advisers were, of course, committed to mouthing a philosophy of
capitalism and free enterprise, so it is not surprising that their plan
was larded with talk about choice and competition and opportunities for initiative. But they were even more deeply committed
to maintaining the status quo, whatever it may be. So in the end
their talk of choice became reminiscent of Henry Ford's pitch
about his Model T: You can have it any color you like as long as
it's black! They were further blinded to the possibility of change
in education by their commitment to hierarchy—in organization,
in epistemology, and in social relations. But calling hierarchy into
question is the crux of the problem of educational change.

Bush's blindness to the real issues was visible in his proposal
to make a grant of a million dollars to each congressional district

in support of an experimental school. At first blush this seems to be aimed at fostering diversity, but it is predictable that the schools selected would be to the liking of the educational establishment, and in any case would not be sufficiently well funded to try anything very new.

A variant on the plan, which would cost the same and might actually work, is a competition to select fifty proposals for experimental schools and give each a grant of ten million dollars, with the judges under orders to encourage diversity. Since the panel of judges would inevitably be dominated by the education establishment, I would expect the first ten or twenty choices to be minor variants on School as we know it. But long before the panel got to its fiftieth choice, it would be forced by its mandate to consider plans that were really different. This variant, however, is only a thought experiment to bring out the weakness of the Bush plan. It is far from what I see as the likely route to educational megachange. On the contrary, this would have to begin much closer to the grass roots.

To create a concrete image of change, imagine an elementary school teacher, let's call her Martha, who reads this book and decides that she would like to follow Thelma's example in her own classroom. Her first problem is to get some equipment. Ten years ago this would have been a main financial problem. In Thelma's case, there was a program that provided computers to participating teachers; other teachers wrote grant proposals, persuaded the school administration, or appealed to parents. But for Martha, School's "immune response" has created a different kind of problem. It is hard for her to get computers because her school has already invested heavily in them and is using them for other purposes—perhaps for drill and practice, perhaps for "computer literacy."

But let us suppose that Martha has solved the equipment problem and is ready to move into action. She now faces another problem, of acquiring a sufficient computer culture to feel confident about guiding her students. Many teachers in Thelma's generation participated in programs whose goals were not merely to provide technical knowledge about computers but to do so in the mathetic spirit that comes through in the vignettes of work in their classrooms. Martha will not find it easy to repeat their learning experience. She will have trouble finding a suitable program. If she finds one she will have trouble convincing her school administration that she should be given the free time needed to participate in it. The administrators will draw her attention to the fact that the school system, or perhaps its computer vendor, provides seminars on "using computers." In a few afternoons teachers learn the essentials of computer literacy. You don't really need a three-week course. Besides, the school has a full-time computer teacher. The administrators at first don't understand her explanation that she wants to do much more than use a computer. But if Martha succeeds in getting the idea across that she is hoping to see children learn math in new ways, she will run up against a new obstacle. She is told that the school has already decided how children should learn math, that it has adopted the XYZ math series, that the district employs a math coordinator to discuss problems, that it is not for her to strike off on new initiatives of her own.

Believe me, this barrage of objections is only a small part of the troubles Martha will encounter in attempting to launch her initiative within her school. What is remarkable is that many like her will actually manage to introduce new methods into their classrooms, though at the cost of dissipating in struggles with the system a large part of the extraordinary fount of energy that caring teachers find in themselves. The problem of channeling this energy more effectively is at the heart of my opening question: What can be done? It is not my intention here to provide a blueprint answer, for I neither believe that there is only one nor accept the idea of being in the position of a supplier (a "guru") to consumers of plans for change. What I shall try to do here is to place myself, as far as I can, in Martha's shoes and think through one example of a concrete plan, as Martha herself might do.

Martha has come to the conclusion that there must be a better plan than tackling the obstacles one at a time. As long as she is an isolated individual in a school of forty teachers and three administrators, such problems will come up over and over again. She believes that she would have the strength to continue to deal with them if there were no other way but has now decided to look for a more systemic approach. Looking around for models she finds three. A first approach, with Project Mindstorm as a model, is to "convert" the school, restructuring its ways of thinking and its forms of organization, not necessarily to conform fully with her own personal vision but sufficiently to provide space for a process in which she can believe. A second approach, based on models like the Costa Rican computer project, is to create a community that cuts across the boundaries of schools. A third approach, on which I will concentrate here, is the "little school" model—a name that comes from the Danish practice of providing government funds to groups of citizens who show themselves to be serious about setting up what in the United States we would call an alternative school.

Martha has read about exciting little schools in Denmark but is able to find out more about models closer to home. In 1968 New York City carried out a formal decentralization of its school system by establishing school districts with a large degree of autonomy over the elementary and junior high schools in their territories. In itself this decentralization remained "formal" and did not give rise to any of the benefits that would come from a true break with centralized organization, largely because it was conceived as reorganizing the centralized bureaucratic system: The districts did not see themselves as challenging centralized authority as such; they saw themselves as acquiring a centralized authority over their own turfs. More recently some of the districts have adopted a policy that takes a more significant step toward a truer decentralization. They have set up a procedure to allow a group of teachers, gener-

Charter schools

ally between six and ten, to submit a proposal to create a separate school with the right to set its own educational policy within guidelines approved by the district's school board.

The little schools are still not examples of megachange. But Martha is not looking for a way to achieve megachange directly. She can see that the development of a megachanged learning environment will have to be a social process that will grow slowly in an organic way. It will involve the growth of a truly different culture of learning, replete with a literature, with jokes, with new ways of thinking about what is to be learned and how to learn it—in short, with much more than Martha and a handful of colleagues can bring about by themselves. The problem she is trying to solve is on another level from making megachange: She is not looking for a way to invent megachange single-handed but to participate in its emergence. She is looking for a way to lead a satisfying life as a teacher and, given who she is, this implies being part of the development of new ways of learning.

In discussing Costa Rica I noted the way in which Logo became a medium for what Bell Hooks, writing about a similar situation in the experience of African-American women, called the recovery of identity. Work with computers became a way for people in a small "underdeveloped" country to lay claim to the tools of the future; it was a way for teachers to reject the definition of their profession as excluding the mastery of anything complex, modern, and technical; and it was a way for women to declare to themselves as much as to others that technology was not something that only men could own. In the United States I have seen Logo used by women in a similar spirit. I have seen children in "special ed" classes use it militantly to assert their real identity against School's classification of them as incompetent. Each of these cases suggests ways in which a little school created in a militant spirit can mobilize technology as an assertion of identity.

In discussing intellectual styles I noted how *bricoleurs* were able to recover a particular kind of identity for which they usually had no name: an epistemological identity, which they had come to feel was inferior and now found to be a source of intellectual power and pride. I am led to reflect on the fact that while many alternative schools define themselves by a domain of interest such as art or writing or science, few explicitly define themselves by an epistemological preference.

The nearest approach I know to this is the Afrocentric school. Of course, in this case there is much more than an epistemology; there is a set of values, a sense of ethnic identity, and perhaps a political position. The one I know best is the Paige Academy in Boston, which adds yet more dimensions through its connections with the surrounding community.

I could continue in this spirit, but this may be enough to make the point that little schools could give themselves a deeper and more conscious specific identity. Everything I have said in this book converges to suggest that this would produce rich intellectual environments in which not only children and teachers but also new ideas about learning would develop together. It is only in such an ecology of mutations and hybridizations of ways of learning that a truly new mathetic culture could emerge. As Darwin taught us to understand, two key ideas that explain biological evolution and many other emergent processes are variation and selection. Although we now know that the process is more complex than Darwin imagined, biological evolution is still seen as dependent on there being ample opportunity for variety. I see little schools as the most powerful, perhaps an essential, route to generating variety for the evolution of education.

The prevailing wisdom in the education establishment might agree with the need for variety but would look to other sources to provide it. For example, many—let us call them the Rigorous Researchers—would say that the proper place for both variation and selection is in the laboratory. On their model, researchers should develop large numbers of different ideas, test them rigorously, select the best, and disseminate them to schools.

In my view this is simply Gosplan in educational disguise. Imagine that you had invented a new device for the kitchen and could demonstrate that ten million people wanted the thing. You would not be able to beat off the rush of would-be backers! Your device would soon be out in the world. Now imagine that you had an idea about education that appealed to twenty or thirty million people—say, to one person in five in every district of the country. Although in many areas of economic competition this would represent a market share beyond the wildest dreams of most entrepreneurs, it still might not be enough to generate a single "sale" to a school board.

The ridiculous situation where supply and demand exist but cannot meet comes from the commitment to uniformity in schools. In most countries the uniformity works at a national level: A ministry of education would have to decide to adopt the new idea. In the United States there is a decentralized system that allows each town to make its own decisions. This makes it easier for some kinds of variety to exist: most easily, educational forms that match the social and class composition of a particular town. But variety on fundamental educational issues is just as effectively stalled by the requirement of majority assent on the level of a town or even of a school as on the level of a nation. The importance of the concept of the little school is that it provides a powerful, perhaps by far the most powerful, strategy to allow the operation of the principle of variation and selection.

The Rigorous Researcher will object to the populist tone of this argument. It is appropriate to buy a food processor or a garlic press on the basis of individual whim, but education is more serious. Every child deserves the best. Science should be used to find out what is the best, and then everyone should adopt the proven methods. Personal decision is simply not appropriate.

This objection depends on an assumption that is at the core of the technicalist model of education: Certain procedures are the best, and the people involved can be ordered to carry them out. But even if there were such a thing as "the best method" for learning, it would still only be the best, or even mildly good, if people (teachers, parents, and learners) believed in it. The bureaucrat thinks that you can make people believe in something by issuing orders. This belief is supported by the rationalist, who believes that you can make people believe in something by advancing convincing arguments. But what if you can't? What if teachers and parents, and even children, persist in having different ideas? Then we have the choice of using force to run the system bureaucratically or reducing it to the common denominator of what everyone can believe. We would have totalitarian education or trivialized education. Indeed, if it were not for the resistance of teachers like Martha, School would not even make the choice but would achieve both—and sometimes it does so despite the Marthas.

A central feature of the little school idea is that it permits a group of like-minded people—teachers, parents, and children— to act together on the basis of authentic personal beliefs. Instead of imposing a common way of thinking on everyone, it allows people with a shared way of thinking to come together. I want to argue that this makes sense even from the point of view of the Rigorous Researcher, who should see that the little school is the most appropriate laboratory for the evolution of methods of learning. This is true, in particular, of a component of children's learning environment that has been given the least attention in this book, namely, parents.

If Martha and her team are really going to explore new ideas, they are likely to act in ways that may go against the grain of how parents think about learning. This is something that can undermine the effectiveness of the little school's work; but if parents understand what is being done at school, supportive discussion at home can very much reinforce it. So the match between parents and the school is also an important factor in how it will develop.

An instructive example of the effect of unfavorable reactions of parents was provided by the "new math" movement that began in the 1960s. The launching of the first earth satellite by the USSR provoked a panic about Soviet superiority in science and technology, and this precipitated a movement of curriculum reform in U.S. schools that eventually spread all over the world. A prominent component of this reform was a new approach to teaching mathematics in elementary school. Teams of mathematicians and psychologists and teachers were brought together to develop the new approach. Under the influence of the mathematicians they decided (correctly) that the traditional teaching of mathematics placed too much emphasis on rote learning, but went on to argue that the remedy was to teach the children the "logic" behind the mathematics. The argument was deeply flawed in a number of ways, of which the most immediately relevant here is that the general public, and that included the vast majority of parents, had little understanding of this new math and even less sympathy for it. Many parents responded by ridiculing what they saw their children doing—hardly a good way to support learning. And even when parents did not actively poke fun at what their children were doing, their incomprehension added to the sense among the children that it was acceptable not to understand math—their parents didn't, and even seemed to be proud of their lack of understanding.

The importance of parents' reactions to mathematics highlights the complexity and delicacy of the social and cultural side of educational change. It also highlights how much this has been neglected by educators: Not only did the new math movement fail to please parents, but the instigators of the movement did not even consider this to be a relevant factor. The discussions preceding the design and adoption of the new curriculum paid much attention to the opinions of mathematicians about what kind of math is "good math," as well as to the opinions of psychologists about what was learnable by children. The discussions paid no attention at all to the cultural side of learning; they did not consider questions about the relationship of the old math or of the new math to the prevailing culture.

Had they done so, this might have had several possible outcomes. At the least, more attention would have been paid to helping parents understand what was being done. It is hard to predict what would have happened in this case. Certainly the response to the new approach would have been somewhat more enthusiastic. In my view it would not have been very much more so, because the conflict between the culture and the new math was too deep to be overcome by good public relations. A more significant possible consequence could have been that the innovators might have come to understand the need to redesign their curriculum to obtain a better cultural resonance. But in either case the story of the new math has a moral for Martha and for those trying to support her efforts: The design of a learning environment has to take account of the cultural environment as well, and its implementation must make serious efforts at involvement of the communities in which it is to operate.

I am not sure that any approach to math reform could have been effective in the 1960s. Fortunately, Martha lives at a time when many factors contribute to richer opportunities for developing a culturally syntonic learning environment. It is instructive for the general problem to review some of the ways in which mathematics can be handled better by little schools that might provide a model for Martha.

One must never get tired of reiterating the obvious: Even if nothing else had changed, the simple fact of being a little school could make a decisive difference if it led to a self-selection of parents who were favorable to its particular educational philosophy. In that case, instead of struggling with a skeptical and distrustful parent body, the school would benefit from the commitment the parents made in selecting the school. Even at the time of the new math movement, an alternative school could have used this factor—and, indeed, some did—to create a better intellectual ambiance. But today a little school can take this advantage much further. The particular innovation made in the new math was isolated in various ways. It was confined specifically to math with a little spillover to science; it was in its nature attractive to a small number of people.

Building its approach to mathematics on the use of computers gives the modern little school a chance to break out of this isolation. Quite independently of its "true" educational value, associating mathematics with computers has a much better chance to elicit positive responses than associating it with an unknown esoteric thing called "set theory." A typical parent's reaction will be much more positive to a child coming home and saying, "I did math with computers," than to, "In math we did set theory." This kind of acceptance of the computer is open to exploitation: All sorts of superficial activities are dressed up as "computer learning." But the fact that poor educational methods can be dressed in computational clothing does not in any way diminish the fact that a favorable attitude to the idea of children learning about computers can be used as a bridge for parents to understand educationally sound work. The parents are predisposed to hear. They are also predisposed to believe that learning about computers leads to learning about mathematics, for it is well established in the public mind that computers are "mathematical." People might not quite know what this means, but it is enough to establish a positive attitude to mathematics through the subject's connection with computers.

A new approach to mathematics through computation reduces isolation in other ways as well, for, as I have repeatedly shown in this book, mathematics is thereby connected with many other domains of interest that parents might understand and care about. This includes specific subjects such as dance, robotics, writing, and social studies; but perhaps even more important, it includes epistemological positions that might appeal to parents through feminist, Afrocentric (and other kinds of multicultural), or environmental connections. Thus there is a basis in principle for the little school to try to develop dialogue with parents on a range of bandwidths.

Of course, there is a big step between the existence in principle of a basis for dialogue and its establishment in a rich form. I am not trying to suggest that this is easy or even that I know how to go about it. My point is simply that a very new opportunity exists for mobilizing a larger public in pursuit of educational change. And it seems to me very clear that a dynamic little school that is itself based on a principled stand on the connecting issues is in a much better position to do this than a cumbersome traditional school.

Another way in which technology will contribute to providing a more favorable environment to the diverse initiatives toward new contexts for learning is through electronic communications. Even if there were many more little schools than exist today, and even if they were bolder and more varied in their innovations, they would not constitute an evolutionary ecology unless they were part of an interacting system. The development of better technologies of communication has a significant contribution to make to the transformation of the command system of School to an initiative system.

New technologies of communication also provide an answer to what some readers might have seen as an objection to the concept of little schools. They might seem to be isolationist, fostering a greater balkanization of communities than exists already. But imagine being able to visit electronically with a school in a virtual reality similar in spirit to the virtual reality in which I was imagining Jennifer visiting giraffes in Africa. Imagine schools from across the world collaborating on projects. Such images suggest opportunities for contact among schools that go far beyond anything known in the past. It is no longer necessary to bring a thousand children together in one building and under one administration in order to develop a sense of community.

This, in turn, means that over time the function of little schools is likely to change. The large schools are too cumbersome to maneuver in the turbulent waters of megachange. My vision is not inconsistent with a scenario in which a little school's movement draws in 10 percent of the children, uses this to blaze a trail toward new ways of learning, but passes out of existence when this catalytic and exploratory function has been served. Yet I do not see this as the most likely scenario, for over the long run it is probable that large schools will cease to be needed at all.

What advantage does the large school have over the little one? Some advantages that existed in the past are destined to vanish. This is most strikingly true of the ability to afford a large library. Few schools have good libraries anyway; but in the electronic era every school, indeed every home, will be able to have distant access to reference books, encyclopedias, and the like, as well as the world's literature without the reader's having to move from armchair or playroom. Likewise, communication technology will expand the opportunity to meet other people of like interests. Even the always more or less illusory belief that in a large school there is a better chance to have a teacher in whatever area might interest an individual student is undermined by the possibility of getting in touch with experts at a distance.

There is only one kind of argument against little schools that troubles me, though not sufficiently for me to abandon the approach. These arguments turn around issues of elitism and of protecting children from exploitation. In principle, the traditional public school has the potential of ensuring equal opportunity for everyone. In principle, the idea of breaking it up into smaller units undermines, if not the potential for protecting children, at least the traditional ways of trying to do so.

In the last analysis my answer to these arguments is that public school has paid the heavy price of bureaucratization without adequately protecting those in greatest need. In this sense there is no substantial objection to answer. The situation once again evokes an analogy with the Soviet economy. The USSR used to boast that all its citizens had jobs and a degree of social security. It proclaimed that it protected everyone. But a terrible price was paid, and not in fact for protection but for the illusion of protection. I do not see that School can be defended in its social role. It does not serve the functions it claims, and will do so less and less.

These functions of social protection of children are certainly needed. It would be heartbreaking to look into the future only to see wonderful networks of access to knowledge for some people while others were excluded, or to see that education had become even more than in the past a breeding ground for intolerance and hatred. The prospect is so grim that I would be reluctant to accept any merely intellectual advantages at the cost of giving up a status quo that served democracy and cultural diversity. But what I am not ready to accept is giving up real advantages in exchange for the pretense of equality. The only rational choice I see is to forge ahead in the encouragement of educational diversity with a dedicated commitment not only to expanding its benefits to all who want them but also to making sure that those who choose not to want them are making an informed choice.

Sources of Information

• • •

Council for Logo in Mathematics Education
10 Bogert Avenue
White Plains, NY 10606
Phone: (914) 946-5143

Epistemology and Learning Group
Media-Lab E15-309
Massachusetts Institute of Technology
20 Ames Street
Cambridge, MA 02139
Phone: (617) 253-7851
Fax: (617) 253-6215

Logo Foundation
250 West 57th Street, Suite 2603
New York, NY 10107-2603
Phone: (212) 765-4918
Fax: (212) 765-4789

Logo Special Interest Group
International Society for Technology in Education
1787 Agate Street

Eugene, OR 97403-1923
Phone: (503) 346-4414
Fax: (503) 346-5890

Sources of Logo Software

Harvard Associates
10 Holworthy Street
Cambridge, MA 02138
Phone: (617) 492-0660
Fax: (617) 492-4610

Lego Dacta
555 Taylor Road
Enfield, CT 06082
Phone: (800) 527-8339
Fax: (203) 763-2466

Logo Computer Systems, Inc.
P.O. Box 162
Highgate Springs, VT 05460
Customer Service: (800) 321-5646
Fax: (514) 331-1380

Paradigm Software, Inc.
P.O. Box 2995
Cambridge, MA 02238
Phone: (617) 576-7675

Terrapin Software, Inc.
400 Riverside Street
Portland, ME 04103
Phone: (207) 878-8200
Fax: (207) 797-9235

Bibliography

• • •

ABELSON, HAL AND ANDREA DISESSA. *Turtle Geometry.* Cambridge, Mass.: MIT Press, 1981.

BECKER, H. D., H. EDEN, AND G. FISCHER. *Interactive Problem Solving Using Logo.* Hillsdale, N.J.: Lawrence Erlbaum Associates, 1991.

CLAYSON, JAMES. *Visual Modeling with Logo.* Cambridge, Mass.: MIT Press, 1987.

CLEMENTS, D. H. AND M. T. BATTISTA. *Logo Geometry.* Morristown, N.J.: Silver Burdett & Ginn, 1991.

FREIRE, PAULO AND DONALDO MACEDO. *Literacy: Reading the Word and the World.* New York: Bergin & Garvey, 1987.

GOLDENBERG, E. PAUL AND WALLACE FEURZEIG. *Exploring Language with Logo.* Cambridge Mass.: MIT Press, 1987.

HAREL, IDIT. *Children Designers: Interdisciplinary Constructions for Learning and Knowing Mathematics in a Computer-Rich School.* Norwood N.J.: Ablex, 1991.

HAREL, IDIT AND SEYMOUR PAPERT, EDS. *Constructionism.* Norwood, N.J.: Ablex, 1991.

HARPER, DENNIS O. *Logo Theory and Practice.* Belmont, Calif.: Brooks/ Cole Publishing Co., 1989.

HARVEY, BRIAN. *Computer Science Logo Style,* 3 vols. Cambridge, Mass.: MIT Press, 1985, 1986, 1987.

HOYLES, CELIA AND RICHARD NOSS. *Learning Mathematics and Logo.* Cambridge, Mass.: MIT Press, 1992.

ILLICH, IVAN. *Deschooling Society.* New York: Harper & Row, 1983.

LATOUR, BRUNO. *Science in Action.* Cambridge, Mass.: Harvard University Press, 1987.

LAVE, JEAN. *Cognition in Practice.* Cambridge: Cambridge University Press, 1988.

LAWLER, ROBERT W. *Computer Experience and Cognitive Development.* New York: John Wiley and Sons, 1985.

McCULLOCH, WARREN. *Embodiments of Mind.* Cambridge, Mass.: MIT Press, 1965.

MADDAX, C. D. *Logo in the Schools.* Redding, Calif.: Hayworth Press, 1985.

MINSKY, MARVIN. *The Society of Mind.* New York: Simon and Schuster, 1986.

PAPERT, SEYMOUR. *Mindstorms: Children, Computers, and Powerful Ideas.* New York: Basic Books, 1980.

———. "Teaching Children Thinking." In *The Computer in the School: Tutor, Tutee, Tool,* ed. Robert P. Taylor. New York: Teachers College Press, 1980.

PECK, M. SCOTT. *The Road Less Traveled.* New York: Touchstone/ Simon and Schuster, 1980.

PIAGET, JEAN. *The Child's Conception of Number.* New York: Norton, [1941] 1965.

———. *The Grasp of Consciousness: Action and Concept in the Young Child.* Cambridge, Mass.: Harvard University Press, [1974] 1976.

RESNICK, MITCHEL. "Beyond the Centralized Mindset." Ph.D. diss., Massachusetts Institute of Technology, 1992.

———. "Xylophones, Hamsters, and Fireworks: The Role of Diversity in Constructionist Activities." In *Constructionism,* ed. Idit Harel and Seymour Papert. Norwood, N.J.: Ablex, 1991.

RESNICK, MITCHEL AND STEPHEN OCKO. "LEGO/Logo: Learning Through and About Design." In *Constructionism,* ed. Idit Harel and Seymour Papert. Norwood, N.J.: Ablex, 1991.

SUPPES, PATRICK. "The Future of Computers in Education." In *The Computer in the School: Tutor, Tutee, Tool,* ed. Robert P. Taylor. New York: Teachers College Press, 1980.

Turkle, Sherry. *The Second Self: Computers and the Human Spirit.* New York: Simon and Schuster, 1984.

Turkle, Sherry and Seymour Papert. "Epistemological Pluralism: Styles and Voices within the Computer Culture." *Signs* 16, no. 1 (1990).

Wiener, Norbert. *Cybernetics: Control and Communication in the Animal and the Machine.* New York: Wiley, 1948.

————. *The Human Use of Human Beings: Cybernetics and Society.* Garden City, New York: Doubleday, 1954.

Index

● ● ●